YOU POSITIVELY C

Jack Crossley spent some 40 years in Fleet Street, first as a reporter on the *Daily Mail* and later as news editor/assistant editor on the *Mail*, the *Observer*, the *Herald* (Glasgow), the *Daily Express*, *The Times* and, for two crazy months, the *National Enquirer* in Florida.

He also edited the *Sunday Standard*, a short-lived quality broadsheet in Scotland, and was briefly a reporter on the Quincy *Patriot Ledger* in Massachusetts.

He now lives in London, with his wife, Kate.

You Positively Couldn't Make It Up

JACK CROSSLEY

You Positively Couldn't Make It Up

**YET MORE
BIZARRE-BUT-TRUE
STORIES**
FROM AROUND BRITAIN

JOHN BLAKE

Published by John Blake Publishing Ltd,
3, Bramber Court, 2 Bramber Road,
London W14 9PB, England

www.blake.co.uk

First published in paperback in 2006

ISBN 1 84454 314 5

British Library Cataloguing-in-Publication Data:

A catalogue record for this book is available from the British Library.

Design by www.envydesign.co.uk

Illustrations by John Miers

Printed and bound in Great Britain by Bookmarque

1 3 5 7 9 10 8 6 4 2

Papers used by John Blake Publishing are natural, recyclable
products made from wood grown in sustainable forests.
The manufacturing processes conform to the environmental
regulations of the country of origin.

Every attempt has been made to contact the relevant copyright-
holders, but some were unobtainable. We would be grateful if the
appropriate people could contact us.

Contents

Introduction

In my day job as a newspaperman I plough through chaotic piles of newspapers and magazines. First, I absorb the serious news. Then I start all over again looking for the ridiculous. I start at 6am and it is often noon before I finish and reach for a large Scotch. Some of the items which make up this book take no more than a couple of minutes.

Others can take half an hour or more – digesting long articles and extracting from them a couple of sentences that throw some light on what it is about the British that make the British British.

Lots of publications have columns of bizarre stories from around the world. You can go mining for them on several internet sites. But when somebody does something barmy in California, that's just barmy Californians being barmy.

I like the people in my books to be the British doing hilarious things and believing that they are totally sane. I believe this about the two brothers who live in a village which has no pub. They drink in a pub in a nearby village. Separately. On alternate nights. Why? 'Because we only have one bike.'

I think I have only used one completely foreign story in my previous volumes. (Mafia hit man tells court he is innocent of the gunning down of a man in New York because he was busy gunning down somebody in Los Angeles on the day in question.) I sometimes think I shouldn't have let it in and am currently trying to fight the temptation to include another in the forthcoming fifth volume: Canadian woman returns home to find a bear eating her porridge.

Each week I aim to produce 1,000 words of British bulldoggery embracing our traditional role of triumphantly muddling through with affable incompetence. Some of these weekly outpourings are available in advance for any publication that would like to join in the game.

Chapter 1

Signs of the Times

Shoe Sale: Buy one. Get one free...

David Frost says the best classified ad he ever read was: 'Unused tombstone for sale. Would suit family called Nesbitt'.

Observer Magazine

Martin Thorp, of Edenbridge, Kent, got a chef's knife as a present with instructions which advised him to 'take the knife handle in your working hand (right for right-handed users, left for left-handed users)'.

'I was laughing so much,' he writes, 'I nearly missed the recommendation to "avoid extending your finger on to the blade".'

The Times

Jon Henley's diary in the *Guardian* reports that a gratifying number of its readers have submitted confirmed sightings of a sign on Penrith railway station reading: 'Keep away from the edge of the platform or you may get sucked off'.

John Preston, of Birmingham, bought a pair of socks from a market trader labelled 'All sizes 7–12'. Inside the pack, he found one size-7 sock and one size-12 sock.

Guardian

'Spring is in the air at last. The bulbs are up and the cemetery is beginning to come to life again'.

Spotted by Vera Wibberley in the
Sheffield General Cemetery Trust magazine

'This space could be yours! Please call the services team'.

Seen in the death notices column of the
Tamworth Times by Jackie Fleming,
of Tamworth, Staffordshire

'Single bed, £15. Can deliver. Replaced by double bed. Yippee!'

Small ad in *Eastbourne & District Advertiser*

Spotted in The Nutshell, Bury St Edmunds, Britain's smallest pub:

> **COACH PARTIES WELCOME**
> **FUNCTION ROOM**
> **AND**
> **DINING AREA**
> For parties of two or less

E. Fletcher, Rochdale, Lancs, *Daily Mail*

'Single mum, 41, own home/car, likes dancing, eating out, pubs, cinema, cosy nights in, seeks simple-minded male'.

Ad spotted by John Chapman,
of Carlisle, in *Cumberland News*

Sign on a meat shop in County Clare: 'Roger your local butcher'.

Spotted by David Briggs, of
Northampton, *Guardian*

Outside a horticultural nursery between Tenby and Pembroke: 'Your fuchsia is in our hands'.

Spotted by Tim Large,
of Reading, *Guardian*

3

'Nissan Micra. P-reg. Purple. 3-door. 50,000 miles. MOT Jan. Lady owner, just been serviced'.

Spotted in a free sheet by James Flanagan, of Manchester, *Daily Mail*

Gwendoline Lane from the Isle of Wight bought a new bathing suit but did not notice, until she got it home, a label which said, 'Material will become transparent in water'.

Daily Mail

Underneath a 'Ladies' toilet sign at Lulworth Cove, Dorset, Tony Johnson, of Rowley Regis, West Midlands, spotted and photographed a waiting bucket.

Daily Mail

An advert in the *Adult Learners' Week* read: 'I want to do be able to help my children to do there homework'.

Spotted in the *Scunthorpe Target* by Malcolm Drakes, of Goxhill, Lincs

An advert announcing immediate openings for security guards said people applying needed to be over twenty-one, have a clean driving licence and 'a limited criminal history'.

Anuradha Koppikar, *Reader's Digest*

'No concert tonight. It was last week'.

Sign spotted by Mrs Joanne Wilkinson outside a concert hall in Conway, North Wales, *Daily Mail*

Snails Lane in Devizes, Wiltshire, has a 5mph speed limit.

Spotted by Mrs D Hague, *Daily Mail*

John Greensmith, of Bristol, saw an item in his local supermarket reduced from £1.79 to £1.78. This was described as a 'Price Smash' and the ticket also boasted 'Save 1p' – 'in case any bargain hunter failed to grasp the magnitude of the saving'.

The Times

Sign in a Bristol shoe shop: 'Shoe sale. Buy one. Get one free'.

Roger Derry, *Reader's Digest*

The instructions that came with a hedge-trimmer bought by Julian Lang, of Aldham, Essex, began with: 'Do not use in the house'.

The Times

A list of notes left for milkmen included:
- **Please close the gate because the birds get in and pick the tops off the bottles.**
- **Leave an extra pint. If this note blows away, please knock.**

5

- Just had a baby. Please leave another one.

Daily Mail

Eddy Fletcher, of Rochdale, Lancashire, spotted this notice at Torquay: 'CANCELLED – No ferries running today. (Wobbly Water)'.

Daily Mail

Quinton Gee spotted this sign at the University of Southampton School of Midwifery: Deliveries at rear of building.

Daily Mail

Bearded lady wanted? Seen in the Personal Ads: 'Widower, late 50s, retired, facially hirsute, smoker, honest, loyal, kind, generous, seeks lady with similar qualities'.

Shropshire Star

In Marple, Stockport, underneath that road sign that shows a bent old couple walking along with the aid of a stick, another sign says: Max Speed 10mph.

Spotted by Conrad Clark of Marple, *Daily Mail*

Polite notice seen in Bowness-on-Windermere by Eddie Clarke of Eastbourne: 'Private Parking. Residents Only. Unauthorised vehicles will be inconvenienced'.

Daily Mail

'*SCRUPLES FOR SALE*' – estate agent's sign outside a house in Tenterden, Kent.

Spotted by Mrs Joan Hillyer of
Littlestone, Kent, *Daily Mail*

Sign spotted by B. C. Ferns, of Reading, on a gate in front of an old cottage in a Buckinghamshire village: 'Young girls wanted for bottling and pickling'.

Daily Mail

Spotted by Anthony Baker of Birmingham: Sign outside a pub near Luton advertising 'Local Lasagne'.

The Times

Spotted in the window of a restaurant in Wimbledon: 'All you can eat with two French tarts. £6'.

S. Scanlon, London SW18, *Reader's Digest*

Spotted in a field in Devon a notice saying: 'On this spot – 1 April 1780 – nothing happened'.

Val Small, Christchurch, Dorset, *Daily Mail*

CAUTION
Floor can be wet
If it has been
RAINING

Seen outside a supermarket in Dewsbury, West Yorkshire: Spotted by Mrs M. Tauzeeh, of Barnet, Hertfordshire, *Daily Mail*

Details of a competition prize included: 'Return flights to Spain. Two nights' accommodation for you and 19 friends in Spain (sharing a double room)'.

Spotted in *Today's Golfer* by
Mr J. M. Brown, Exeter

Bath's well-known department store offered Jolly funerals.

Peter Chapman, Bridgend,
Glamorgan, *Guardian*

Edenbridge Strollers – Circular walk from Chiddingstone Causeway. Meet at Leisure Centre 9.30am. Bring cars.

Spotted in the *Tandridge Chronicle* by
Mrs J. Reid, Lingfield, Surrey

The Lonely Hearts ads in the *London Review of Books* has a cult following. Lonely intellectuals send in off-the-wall ads such as:

• Beneath this hostile museum curator's exterior lurks a hostile museum curator's interior.
• Male, 32, looking for a woman with knowledge of advanced humanoid circuit systems.
• Greetings, Earthlings – I have come to infest your puny body with legions of my spawn.

LRB's editor says the magazine is 'a home for a

particular level of intellectual engagement – but also people like to be silly every now and again'.

The Times

At a Burns Night dinner raffle Mrs D. G. Golubovas of Canterbury won a haggis labelled 'Made in Korea'.

Daily Mail

Which? magazine asked its readers to send in examples of peculiar labels. Favourites included:

- A birthday card for 2-year-olds warning that it was not suitable for children under 3.
- A torch labelled 'to be used in the dark'.
- A tin of yacht varnish 'not suitable for marine use'.
- A box of trainers labelled 'Average contents two'.
- A notice on a door saying: 'Use only when Entering/Exiting'.

Daily Telegraph

Sarah Stroud, of Esher, Surrey, came across a tin of throat lozenges in her room at a Shanghai hotel with a label saying they were 'useful for those infested with "severe halitosis, excessive smokers, drinkers and public relations speakers"'.

The Times

Erica Jones noted that her bicarbonate of soda was labelled 'Best Before 4 October 3118'.

'Pah!' responded Stephanie Darby. 'My mother's bicarb is "Best Before 6 September 5070".'

Daily Telegraph

P. Roberts, of Northolt, Middlesex, expressed his horror on going to Ealing Hospital for an operation assessment and seeing a poster in the reception area reading: 'Thieves operate in this area'.

Daily Telegraph

Ealing Hospital is fortunate to have thieves operating. My local hospital warns: 'Guard dogs operate here'.

Christopher Bolton, Glossop, Derbyshire,

Daily Telegraph

A Health and Safety Executive poster on how to use a ladder says the first thing you should do is 'Face the ladder'.

Nigel Hawkins, Hatfield, Herts, *Daily Telegraph*

A road sign in Durham City reads:
- Police Station
- Courts
- Durham Prison

Spotted by Ian R. Lawton, of Wakefield,
West Yorkshire, who raises the comment:
'Swift Justice?' *Daily Mail*

'Obesity Awareness Class for Overweight Ladies. Every Wednesday. Limited Spaces Available'.

Spotted in the *Newcastle Advertiser* by Sandra Heath, Newcastle-under-Lyme, Staffordshire

'A North Essex charity offering help on obesity problems is looking to expand'.

BBC Radio Essex

EXPERIENCED
SIGN MAKER
REQUIRED
APPLY WITH IN

Seen in East London by Steve Parsall of E4, who comments, 'Let's hope spelling is part of the job description.'

Daily Mail

Sign on garage door next to Harpsden Church near Henley on Thames: 'Thou shalt not park in thy neighbour's space'.

Henley Standard

Chapter 2

Best of Britishness

Page 3 girls 'a British institution'...

The British are never funnier than when they are miserable, according to a book on comedy which says, 'British humour is frequently melancholic, probably because of the weather, sexual repression and resentment at the class system'. Some examples:

- Morecambe – a cemetery with the lights left on.
- Brighton – looks like it is helping the police with their enquiries.
  (Keith Waterhouse)
- Tell someone that you live, or have lived, in Leeds and they are quite likely

13

to say: 'Well, it's easy to get out of.'
(Alan Bennett on his home town)

- An archaeologist is the best husband a woman can have; the older she gets, the more interested he is in her.
(Agatha Christie)

- Last year my wife ran off with the fellow next door and, I must admit, I miss him.
(Les Dawson)

Daily Mail, excerpts from *Funny You Should Say That*, by Andrew Martin (Penguin)

Peter Corrigan, raconteur, boulevardier and witty chief sports columnist on the *Independent on Sunday*, wrote about The Great British Loser: 'Our major games – football, cricket and both codes of rugby – were created in public houses... But, for decades, rival nations have been beating us at all of them. The fact that the sporting world is still playing to rules devised well over a century ago by Britons who were probably half-pissed at the time is something of which to be genuinely proud'.

Britons have never been any good at summer. They endure it with stoicism rather than adapting to it. When we had an empire, the Briton abroad demonstrated his contempt for warm weather by dressing for dinner and maintaining sartorial standards. The thought of British men in their summer clothes is perhaps the only thing that makes the clouding over of the sky remotely bearable.

Sunday Telegraph

The unpredictability of our climate builds character. We talk about it because it has made us what we are – a country whose national costume is the pullover and whose symbol is as much the umbrella as the sword.

Roy Hattersley, *Daily Mail*

It was Lord Byron who said that the British winter finished at the end of July, recommencing at the beginning of August.

Sunday Telegraph

There's not a word of truth in all that business about Englishmen being reserved and having stiff upper lips. A worldwide survey by some 84 psychologists, published in the *Science* journal, found the English among the most extroverted and open to new experiences. *The Times* carried the story under the headline: 'Steady on, we Brits are really quite exciting'.

Napoleon called Britain a nation of shopkeepers. The Centre for Retail Research calls us a nation of shoplifters. It claims we are the worst in Europe, stealing £3.58 billion worth of goods in 2004.

The Times

Many Brits are irritated at being told to 'have a nice day'. Gerry Hanson, former chairman of the Campaign for Courtesy, wrote to *The Times*, saying that it was 'infinitely preferable to the surly grunt we frequently receive'. Nevertheless, he did enjoy Peter Ustinov's response: 'Thank you, but I have other plans'.

The Times

Another thing that irritates us is cyclists on pavements. But there's nothing new about it. Mr David Schreiber tells *The Times* of the days in the 1920s when his grandfather was arrested for cycling on a pavement in Ipswich. Two weeks later, his grandfather was appointed chief constable of Ipswich and the policeman who made the arrest was up for interview. The young bobby was shaking with fright – until he found himself being greeted with smiling congratulations.

Foreigners applying to become British citizens will have to take a 'Britishness' test. Among things they will be expected to know is in which part of the UK Geordie is spoken – though they will not necessarily be expected to understand it.

Daily Telegraph

A flurry of surveys in 2005 claimed that:

- Britons spend an average of thirty months of their lives behind the wheel of a car. *The Times*
- The average human is capable of enjoying orgasms lasting sixteen hours – spread over a lifetime of seventy-eight years. *Sun*
- We spend six months in the lavatory – and the same time in traffic jams. *Daily Mail* (which also had a headline saying: 'Stop moaning about the housework. It only takes four years').
- The average woman preparing to go out takes ninety minutes to get from shower to front door. *Daily Telegraph.*

Commenting on this last item, a *Daily Telegraph* reader wrote saying that he had a wife and three adult daughters and could 'only assume that the women taking part in the survey were responding to an emergency'.

Britain was voted the world's favourite country in a survey of 26,000 people in 35 countries. The Nations Brand Index found UK citizens the most polite and the best educated. The French were named the world's rudest and Americans were labelled the most ignorant. Sadly, the Brits earned another title: The Most Boring.

Daily Mail

Americans are ignorant, Russians violent, Italians fun. Britons are intelligent, polite, trustworthy, honest – and a bit boring. So says a global survey of the images of ten leading countries as perceived by each other's people.

Observer

The British like to regard themselves as tolerant, honest, law abiding and considerate. But a *Times* report on a poll commissioned by the Home Office concluded that 'we are a race of liars and hypocrites who piously condemn disrespectful behaviour in others, then promptly misbehave ourselves'. We make obscene gestures at other motorists, drop litter, swear in the street, jump queues and keep things we find instead of handing them into the police.

Madonna's American fans are turning away from her – because she has become 'too English'. Her new single 'Sorry', which topped the charts in Britain in March 2006, stalled at number 58 in the US.

The *Sunday Telegraph* reported that, with a country estate in Wiltshire and 'a taste for Timothy Taylor's real ale', Madonna has become the epitome of the English lady of the manor. The report showed her shaking hands with the Queen, learning to shoot and pulling a pint in a pub.

These days, St George's Day seems to consist of moaning that we don't observe it. Good. We shouldn't celebrate Englishness, because national celebrations are for nations that are chippy and insecure... Ignoring St George's Day with cool reserve would be a far more confident expression of Englishness.

Patrick West in *The Times* 'Thunderer' column on 22 April 2005 – the day before St George's Day

It surprises (and disappoints) many people that St George's Day is so poorly celebrated in England. George Courtauld wrote a book to illustrate that 'nevertheless there is an enormous and uplifting groundswell of people who are intensely proud of being English'. He was horrified by reports that many children had no idea that there had been two World Wars, or even one – and that an Anglican bishop had banned the hymn 'I Vow To Thee My Country' in his churches.

Mr Courtauld produced *The Pocket Book of Patriotism*, which was shunned by publishers who disapproved of the use of the 'outdated, provocative, incendiary word "Patriotism" in the title'. So he published the book privately and, within a very short time, sold 150,000.

Daily Mail

The average British shopper spends 273 days of his or her life in queues.

Daily Mail

Tea is regarded as the British answer to everything from tired feet to bereavement. Amid stories that it might be losing its appeal to young people, British newspapers rushed to defend the cuppa, reminding us that, on average, every person in Britain drinks three cups a day – a daily total of 165 million cups a year. *The Times*, on its influential leader page, thundered: 'Tea drinking is a national ritual as quintessential as keeping a stiff upper lip'.

Churchill realised that tea was crucial to Britain's war effort and during World War II stockpiles were kept at 500 secret locations.

Labour veteran Tony Benn claimed that he used to drink a pint of tea every hour.

Victorian Prime Minister William Gladstone filled his hot water bottle with tea so he could have a cuppa during the night. *The Times/Sun*

Tea is a drink which unites all of England. Butlers serve it to dukes and duchesses, who drink it from china cups. The upwardly mobile middle classes sip it with their little fingers pointing in the air. It finds its finest expression in transport cafes, where it is the colour of mud and tastes best with bacon sandwiches.

Roy Hattersley, *Daily Mail*

Builder's tea comes in a mug – preferably chipped. It should be the colour of wet sand – capable of stripping and staining teeth. Preferably taken with heaped teaspoons of sugar and dollops of full-fat milk. Tetley use thirty-two teas from around the world to get builder's tea just right. It takes a taster five years to learn how to get that exact oily taste, dusty thickness and dirty brick colour.

Daily Telegraph

One company has applied to register 'Builder's Tea' as a trademark. A spokesman said, 'It will be at the stronger end of the palate. It's not a Darjeeling – put it that way.' Ah, well... as long as the teaspoon stands up in it.

Daily Telegraph

Henley Regatta is 'one of the few places left in Britain where standards are still maintained'.

Regatta fan Garry Hunt said this to *Guardian* writer Mark Honigsbaum as a punt floated by with its passengers sipping Pimms to the accompaniment of 'Teddy Bears' Picnic'.

'See what I mean,' said Mr Hunt. 'Where else would you come across such a quintessential British scene?'

'And there's no spitting or foul language,' said Mrs Hunt.

Honigsbaum writes, 'Ever since 1839 the event has attracted rowing enthusiasts and the public – united in their love of British fair play and traditional, if eccentric, dress.'

The Guardian man was told by an 82-year-old about the days when only men were allowed to compete and about the year the Russians won but were not allowed to hoist their national flag.

Guardian

In a truly British dispute, a minority of some twenty-five owners of allotments at New Aspley, Nottingham, refused a developer's offer of up to £28,000 each for plots which had originally cost them as little as £100. 'We would rather carry on with life's enjoyments,' they said.

Daily Telegraph

The *Telegraph* followed this up with a leader saying: 'We fully understand how exasperating these people must be to the majority who want to sell... But there is something admirable about a bloody-minded Briton who knows his rights and refuses to give them up under pressure from a majority.'

The *Daily Mail's* Michael Leapman – an allotment addict – wrote, 'Let's have three cheers for the Aspley 25... Allotments are as much a part of our heritage as stately homes, stone circles and historic gardens... Their sheds, patched up with whatever scrap materials are available, reinforce an impression of desolation – but this is what the British do best. We improvise. We muddle through.'

Daily Mail

The *Daily Telegraph* produced a two-page spread on 'What does it mean to be British?'. A YouGov poll asked people if they believed that Britain had been a force for good in the world: 80% said yes; 50% said they were very proud to be British and 36% were fairly proud. A selection of the great and the good were interviewed about Britishness and they came up with:

- We are the most constitutionally mature.
- We were the first to have an industrial revolution and we don't lose wars.
- We have a deep love of animals and an ambivalence towards children.
- The British don't have an obvious set of values other than their knack of self-deprecation.
- Britain is all about curries, roasts, toast, kettles, gardens, gnomes, tea cosies, rain and the Queen and her corgis.

Daily Telegraph

The next day the *Telegraph* had a piece reminding us that George Orwell once said, 'Nearly every Englishman of working-class origin considers it effeminate to pronounce a foreign word correctly.' But he reserved a special contempt for the 'aitch-pronouncing class'.

William Jackson, of Tonbridge, Kent, responded to the Telegraph's report on Britishness by remembering that Cecil Rhodes said that to be born British was 'to win first prize in the lottery of life'.

B. H. Jackson, of Sheffield, wrote in to the *Telegraph* to say that when he was young to be born in England was a privilege, but it was God-given to be born in Yorkshire.

Britain wins top marks for mediocrity. Headline in The Times over a story on the 2006 edition of the *Economist Pocket World in Figures*, which reports:

- UK's position in the Quality of Life League Table is 29th – behind Slovenia and just ahead of South Korea.
- We are only the sixth biggest drinkers, well behind Luxembourg.
- We are in 31st place when it comes to life expectancy – 79 years, compared with Andorra's 83.5.
- In the road accidents league, we are 25th among the most dangerous countries in the world – marginally better than Slovenia, but riskier than Bolivia.

- English women are only the world's 23rd most obese.

The Times comments, 'However highly the British may rate themselves, it is other countries who lead the way in the health, leisure and business stakes'.

The *Sun's* Page 3 girls have been declared a British institution. In a poll to find our top-ten national treasures – by internet firm Yahoo! – the bare-breasted beauties came sixth. No. 1 was the Sunday roast. No. 2 was regional dialects, with brown sauce coming in at 7 and beer bellies at 8.

Sun

British homes are bursting with gadgets worth a total of £9.4 billion that are rarely, if ever used. The sandwich toaster tops the list with 45% saying they own one, but do not use it. Bathroom scales (31%) are followed by the coffee machine (30%), foot spa (22%) and electric knife (21%).

ICM poll commissioned by esure.com,
Daily Telegraph

Philip Howard's entertaining, idiosyncratic column on modern manners in *The Times* had a reader who asked, 'If another man insults me and refuses to apologise, what is the modern-day equivalent of seeking satisfaction, given that pistols and swords are outlawed? Would a mutual agreement to indulge in fisticuffs put us in trouble with the police?'

Philip replies, 'The police cannot object to a mutually agreed bout providing it is conducted under the Queensbury rules (or thereabouts) and is properly supervised. Or, if punched in private, provided that it does not excite attention or alarm the innocent passing trade. The Brits are notoriously susceptible to violence, when in drink or provoked by an apparent insult. Violence shows that the insulter has wounded you, and therefore he has won. Wit shows that you are above such childish, chav behaviour.'

A quintessentially English battle was harder fought than the 2005 Test matches against Australia. It was the war between two of the prettiest towns in England to win the Thames and Chiltern section of Britain in Bloom. Civic pride took a battering when Henley, the perennial champions, lost the title to its arch-rival Marlow.

A supporter of victorious Marlow said, 'Of course, Henley is ONE of the jewels of the Thames. But we're the one called THE jewel of the Thames.'

A Henley woman said, 'It's like a sibling rivalry, we're always squabbling. Both towns are very similar – but we've got the bigger Waitrose.'

The Times

The *Pocket Book of Patriots* by George Courtauld (Ebury) reports:

- Anthony Trollope worked for the Post Office and invented the pillar-box. He forced himself to write for three hours a day, even on horseback. He designed a desk which clipped on to his saddle when out inspecting post offices.
- Dr Johnson, author of the great *English Dictionary*, was dogged by money troubles. When asked about the finances of a particular project, he said he had 'two very cogent reasons for not printing any list of subscribers. One – I have lost the names. Two – I have spent all the money.'
- Sir Isaac Newton came up with the idea of gravity, discovered the binominal theorem, integral and differential calculus, computed the area of the hyperbola and became an MP and Master of the Royal Mint. He also invented the cat flap.

Daily Mail

One has to tread carefully when daring to interfere with some of the sacred pleasures of the British. Such a treasure is *The Archers*, an everyday story of country folk and the longest-running radio soap in the world. In 2005, The Archers programme was attracting big audiences with the drama of Emma's baby. Was the father her husband, Will Grundy – or her husband's brother, Ed Grundy? Such was the intensity of interest that newspapers published photographs of the actors involved.

Charlotte Garnett, of Haslemere, Surrey, fired a blast in the letters column of the Daily Telegraph, demanding: 'Please stop showing us pictures of The Archers' characters. You listen to a radio play or soap so that you can imagine the characters... The reality of Ed and Will Grundy is a horrid shock and one would have preferred to do without... I can't imagine many girls longing to make it as far as the local church to nab Ed... He looks as though he's never lifted as much as a weeding trowel... How can people be encouraged to use their imaginations if you go and spoil it?'

In August 2005, Harvey Bennett put a message in a bottle and launched it off Long Island, New York. In February 2006, he got a letter from England saying, 'I recently found your bottle while taking a scenic walk on a beach by Poole Harbour. While you may consider this some profound experiment on the path and speed of ocean currents, I have another name for it – litter. You Americans don't seem to be happy unless you are mucking up somewhere'.

BBC News

It was a story that could have been described as bad news for Britain. University research found that the UK was only eighth in an international IQ league – below Germany at 107, Netherlands 107, Poland 106, Sweden 104, Italy 102, Austria 101, and Switzerland 101. But UK newspaper readers rejoiced over the fact that Britain's score of 100 was well above that of the French (19th in the list with 94).

The Times

The *Ocean Villa* cruiseship brochure for Germans had men and women naked in its sauna. For the British brochure, computer wizardry was used to put discreet black swimwear on the naughty nudes. 'The move to stop Brits getting hot under the collar reinforces stereotypes about our reserves, compared to our more forthright Teutonic cousins.'

Daily Mail

Sporting Life

**'I didn't sleep with seven Miss Worlds.
It was only four.' George Best...**

'The goals made such a difference to the way the game went.'

Another gem from football pundit John Motson.
The Times

Radio 5 Live listeners voted this the best sporting commentary of all time:

Jonathan Agnew and Brian Johnston were commentating on a Test match against the West Indies in 1991 when Ian Botham lost his balance and then knocked the bails off when trying to step over his stumps.

Agnew said, 'He couldn't quite get his leg over.'

Both commentators then dissolved into helpless laughter, which went on and on and on as Johnston struggled to carry on reading the score card with tears streaming down his face. He pleaded to the still-giggling Agnew: 'Do stop it, Aggers.'

The tape of the long, drawn-out mirth became an instant radio classic and is used by a London drama school as an example of what not to do when overcome by the giggles.

Guardian

Also in Radio 5 Live's shortlist of best sporting commentaries was BBC's Peter Bromley describing Shergar winning the Derby in 1981: 'You need a telescope to see the rest.'

Guardian

'I knew how good Sean Murphy was – but I didn't know he was this good.'
Veteran snooker ace and commentator
Willie Thorne on the young outsider who won the
2005 World Snooker Championships, *Sun*

The breasts of Mrs David Beckham 'look like two cupcakes nailed to an ironing board'. Jordan's look like she's keeping a couple of footballs warm under her jumper.

Jan Muir, *Daily Telegraph*

After Victoria Beckham was quoted as saying that she had never read a book, *Guardian* reader Rachel Grunert, of Berkhamsted, Hertfordshire, wrote, 'Presumably this includes her autobiography – in which case she is to be commended for her excellent judgement.'

England's legendary cricket umpire David Shepherd is superstitious. On Friday the 13th, he ties a matchstick to a finger so that he is touching wood all day.

The Times

As the 2005 cricketing battle for the Ashes got under way – with the Australians gaining an early victory in the first Test – the *Daily Mail* reported how British expats often complained about being called 'whingeing Pommy bastards'.

The Australian press response was to accuse the English of being whingeing Pommy bastards for complaining about being called whingeing Pommy bastards.

Daily Mail

In 1984, footballer George Best served two months in jail after being found guilty of charges involving drink-driving and resisting arrest. In the canteen at Southwark Crown Court, his friends and defence team were staring into the bottom of their coffee cups with nothing to say. George glanced at them with a smile and said, 'Well, I suppose that's the knighthood fucked.'

Guardian

They say I slept with seven Miss Worlds. I didn't. It was only four. I didn't turn up for the other three.

George Best, quoted in the *Independent*

When taking down Best's mobile phone number, reporter Sue Mott said, 'God, do you realise half the women in the world would pay good money to get this number?'

Best replied, 'Half the women in the world have got it.'

Independent

Best is reported to have said that Kevin Keegan was not fit to lace his boots. Football writer John Roberts said Keegan was not fit to lace Best's drinks.

Independent

A Glasgow court delayed sentencing a car thief to enable him to watch a vital Rangers match.

Independent on Sunday

The swimming stage of the Visit Scotland Adventure Triathlon required 100 international athletes to plunge into Loch Ness – each one of them insured for £1 million against being bitten by the monster.

Guardian

Modern Wimbledon tennis stars can look forward to becoming millionaires, but this was far from the case for Phyllis King, 99, Wimbledon's oldest surviving champion. She won the doubles with Dorothy Shepherd-Barron in 1931 – and got a £10 shopping voucher which had to be spent on a luxury, not on a 'domestic necessity'. Phyllis added her Wimbledon prize to vouchers won at other tournaments until she had £130 worth – and then bought a Morris Minor.

Daily Mail

When Mark Bolt caught a carp weighing over 50lb in 1995, he was photographed with the monster and then, like all good anglers, gently returned the fish to its lake in Warmwell, Dorset. The carp was one of Britain's most famous fish and anglers knew him as Herman and also as the Warmwell Whacker. Two years after Mark Bolt caught him, Herman died and was stuffed and framed, and put up for auction in Dorchester in 2005.

Herman fetched a whopping £2,234 and was knocked down to... Mark Bolt, 37. 'I had to get him,' said Mark. 'It is a dream come true.'

Daily Mail

As England was spun into a cricketing frenzy during the 2005 Ashes a *Daily Telegraph* leader reminded its readers of the view held by George

Bernard Shaw: 'The English are not a very spiritual people, so they invented cricket to give them some idea of eternity.'

Cricket has the image of being a gentleman's sport watched by well-behaved spectators. But some cricketers indulge in the slightly unsporting practice of 'sledging', in which fielders close to the batsman try to put him off by mumbling unpleasantnesses, *sotto voce*. This example of sledging was given in an *Observer* guide for cricket beginners:

Australian fast bowler to somewhat substantial English batsman: 'Why are you so fat, mate?'

Batsman: 'Because every time I sleep with your wife she feeds me biscuits.'

WF Deedes recalls the days when Warwick Armstrong's Australian XI was 'not particularly gracious' when it was here in 1921. 'I was taken as a small boy to see them at the Oval. My solitary recollection is of seeing Armstrong in the outfield reading an evening newspaper that had blown across the ground.'

Daily Telegraph

Amid the fever that accompanied England's triumphs in the 2005 Test matches against Australia, cricket fanatic and former Prime Minister Sir John Major revealed that he had once penned this ode:

Oh Lord, if I must die today,
Please make it after close of play.
For this I know, if nothing more,
I will not go, without the score.

   Sir John wrote in *The Times* that 2005's Test teams had 'some of the greatest talents in world cricket of whom, one day, old men, now small boys, will babble in awe'.

The Times

England won the Ashes in September 2005 when cricket, long regarded by many as fogeyish and arcane, joyfully gripped the land.

- In the parks of England there have not been many boys kicking footballs... It has been the thwock of bat on ball that has been heard, along with piping cries of 'Howzat'.
- Vicars have been working cricket metaphors into their sermons.
- Sermons have been rather shorter on recent Sundays.
- Retail tills went much quieter as people stayed in to watch on TV.
- Trevor Bish-Jones, chief executive of Woolworth, said, 'Giving up a few sales to beat the Australians seems well worth it to me.'
- Actor and writer Michael Simkins said, 'The England side has shown an

understated Englishness which fits in
with how the nation feels.'

Sunday Telegraph

However, the euphoria which engulfed England over its Ashes victory did not bring much joy to some Scottish hearts. Christine Grahame, an SNP member of the Scottish Parliament, lodged a motion lamenting the BBC's 'overwhelming UK-wide coverage of a sport of marginal interest in Scotland'.

Scotsman

But Press coverage of the SNP whinge was dwarfed by a story involving some of Scotland's enthusiastic 12,000 cricketers. The Crathie Cricket Club – which plays at Balmoral Castle and whose patron is Prince Philip – was suffering a mysterious and calamitous loss of bowling form, winning only two home games all season.

It was not until the last game of the season that someone said, 'This pitch is not the right bloody length.'

It turned out to be 22 metres instead of 22 feet. After that, Crathie won their last match and Prince Philip was reported to have found the whole saga 'hilarious'.

Daily Telegraph

The story on Crathie cricket was followed by a letter from Reginald Wycherley, of Shrewsbury, saying he was sorry that the club managed only two wins at home, but the photograph of their team indicated that they had a slight disadvantage. It showed ten men and two labradors. 'I would have been inclined to field two retrievers,' said Mr Wycherley.

Daily Telegraph

All was not gloom on the Scottish sporting front, however. While the England cricket team had a triumphal parade through London, the folk north of the border were able to celebrate winning the World Elephant Polo Championship for the second consecutive year. They scored a golden goal in a hard-fought tournament in Thailand and their captain, the Duke of Argyll, said, 'The team is ecstatic.'

The Times

Ian Stirling, of Reading, Berkshire, wrote how he dragged his wife from the ironing to see the Test highlights, including a spectator holding up a sign reading: 'I missed my wedding to see this'.

The Times

Ian du Pre, of Kensington, London, wrote how he could imagine nothing more British than being at the Royal Albert Hall's Promenade Concert when news of the Test victory came over the speaker

39

system. 'Foreign tourists looked bemused at the spontaneous roar and the applause and I would swear that a smile came over the face of the bust of Sir Henry Wood.'

The Times

Coverage of the Test matches spilled over from the sports pages onto page one and even into the comment columns of the serious 'heavies'. The *Daily Telegraph* editorialised on 'the almost unbearable tension... this gripping series... sporting drama at its height... England must avoid defeat in the final Test at the Oval. They have the skill and strength of character to do it... The prospect is mouthwatering.'

Daily Telegraph

The *Sun* could not resist having a joke at the expense of the defeated team.

An Aussie batsman, given out LBW by the umpire, said to the man in the white coat, 'That was never LBW – you need glasses.'

The man replied, 'So do you, mate. I'm selling ice creams.'

Ashes hero Andrew ('Freddy') Flintoff was given the freedom of his home town Preston in Lancashire. His teammate Steve Harmison wrote in the *News of the World*, 'Apparently it allows him to drink a pint of beer at forty-eight pubs in the city and get a lift home in a police car without being arrested. Maybe that's a privilege that should be granted to Fred all over the country.'

News of the World

Perhaps just to prolong Australia's agony over losing the Ashes in 2005, the Royal Mail produced a set of postage stamps showing the England team rejoicing. Two of them were 68p stamps – the amount it costs to send a letter to Oz.

The Times

Children taking part in the British Junior Conker Championships on the Isle of Wight in October 2005 were banned from bringing their own conkers to avoid them being doctored with varnish or vinegar, or by baking. Contestants had the option of wearing goggles.

Guardian

Fifty contestants with more than 500 conkers took part in a battle presented by Sompting Village Morris Men at the Ship & Anchor in Ford, West Sussex. Ready-strung conkers were provided to avoid cheating. Arundel Brewery donated a prize for the most bruised knuckles.

West Sussex Gazette

Despite a run of newspaper stories about conkers being a dangerous game, the heroic British team went into battle on the village green in Ashton, Northamptonshire, and beat the world.

Calum Owen, 31, from Selby, North Yorkshire, won the World Conker Championships, having conquered competitors from Russia, Australia, Ukraine, Italy, South Africa and New Zealand.

Jayne Coddington, 43, a legal executive from Boston, Lincolnshire, was women's champion.

The Times

Does the fearsome pre-match Haka performed by New Zealand's rugby team scare other teams or simply embarrass them? Either way, Bob Duffield, of London, SW19, believes it is time for the English team to face down any intimidation 'with our traditional, but equally unsettling, Morris dance'.

The Times

Reg Cave, from Dwygyfylchi, Conwy, Wales, felt a bit intimidated when he walked into a bar in Canada. There were several guys in trapper gear wearing Bowie knives and carrying rifles. On the veranda, one of them was skinning a large bear.

'Where are you from?' he was asked.

'Liverpool.'

'Geeezzz. One hell of a tough town, that. I was lucky to get out alive.'

It turned out that the tough lumberjack had gone to a Liverpool match wearing a Manchester United scarf — which the Anfield fans burned.

Daily Mail

The minnow that Dr Mark Everard caught in a pond in Wiltshire was only four and a half inches long and weighed only half an ounce. But it made headline news because it broke the minnow record and, said Dr Everard, 'fought a battle of Hemingway proportions'.

The Times

For the benefit of England football fans flocking to Germany for the 2006 World Cup, the thoughtful British Embassy in Berlin compiled a list of useful phrases. They include the German for:

Known to the police.

A game of two halves.

Knocked out on penalties.

And, if the result makes them feel sick: parrot.

Sunday Times

London's Goethe Institute offered language lessons for the 2006 World Cup in Germany. It included teaching England supporters key words such as 'tor' (goal), 'eckball' (corner) and 'elfmeter' (penalty). Also available: tuition in German football chants and insults to the referee. Among the useful phrases: 'Der Schiedsrichter braucht 'nen Blindenhund' (the referee needs a guidedog).

The Times

Sir, As any English gentleman will tell you, there are only three sports – hunting, fishing and shooting. The rest are games.

Letter from Walter Wigilmast, Kingston-upon-Thames,
The Times

Former world champion darts player Bobby George starred in ITV's *Celebrity Fit Club* and in January 2006 got his weight down to 16st 1lb – 'way below what is generally regarded on the darts circuit as a man's ideal fighting weight'.

Giles Smith, *The Times*

Millions of TV viewers used to watch the dubious 'sport' of all-in wrestling on Saturday afternoons during the 1960s and 1970s. Jackie Pallo was one of the big stars and told of screaming women spectators being known as 'ring rats'. They used to plunge hat pins into his bottom and stub cigarettes out on his body.

Pallo died in February 2006, aged 79, and is remembered for telling one of the women who loved to hate him: 'Go and live in India, darling – you'd be sacred over there.'

Daily Telegraph

The building of the new Wembley Stadium was well behind schedule and well above budget when *The Times* ran a headline in March 2006: 'Wembley Finally Finished'. Sadly, the story was referring to a Lego version, which took three weeks to build and was made up of 10,000 toy bricks.

However, fans hungry for news about the beleaguered real thing may have got some consolation from this report: The new Wembley Stadium will have more toilets than any other building on Earth (2,618 of them) and will indeed be a fitting home for English football.

David Randall, *Independent on Sunday*

Harry Pope, of Eastbourne, tells how he visited a Harry Secombe charity cricket match in the 70s. He and his father were perched on two stools in the bar and got into conversation with Hattie Jacques. Harry offered Hattie his stool and the well-built actress gave him an icy stare and said, 'I am already sitting on one.'

Daily Mail

'Are there any changing facilities?'

Chapter 4

Law & Disorder

It is still OK to shoot a Welshman with a longbow – but only on a Sunday…

Patrick Pakenham died aged 68 in June 2005. He was a talented barrister and his exuberant behaviour made him something of a legend. The *Daily Telegraph*'s obituary recounted one of his exploits at the bar.

Pakenham was appearing before an irascible judge in a drugs case. The evidence included a bag of cannabis and the judge, considering himself an expert, asked for the bag to be passed up to him. He opened the package, inserted some of the contents into his mouth, chewed it and announced, 'Yes, it is cannabis. Where was the substance found, Mr Pakenham?'

The reply came swiftly, if inaccurately: 'In the defendant's anus, my Lord.'

Daily Telegraph

Excuses offered by people caught not having a TV licence include:
- **Only the dog watches it.**
- **That's not a TV – it's a fish tank.**
- **I never use my set – I just switched on *EastEnders* to see if it affected my radio reception.**
- **I'm too busy having sex with my wife.**
- **I watch only Australian soaps and they don't have to have a licence over there.**

The Times

Warmest congratulations to police in Sutton's Worcester Park area who, after a surveillance operation, amassed enough evidence to shut down a local crack house. The property is located above Worcester Park police station – but splendid work for all that.

Guardian/Surrey Online

Schoolboy Michael Fishpool was hauled before Teesside Youth Court for riding his battery-powered scooter without insurance or a driving licence when he was 12

years old. He received six penalty points which will be wiped from his record in June 2008 – when he will still be too young to apply for a provisional car licence.

Daily Mail

Nick Lenthall beeped his council lorry's horn at seven policemen manning a speed trap near Bournemouth. He was followed by ALL of them and fined £30 'for unnecessary use of audible warning equipment'.

Sun – in part of its 'You Couldn't Make It Up' series

Teresa Webb, 30, was given an ASBO (Anti-Social Behaviour Order) by Bath and N. E. Somerset Council for repeatedly playing the hit single 'Is This The Way To Amarillo'. Bath magistrates ruled that the music had caused harassment, alarm or distress.

Daily Mail/Telegraph

Terry Bearpark, 20, downed a burglar by hitting him on the head with a shovel. At Teesside Crown Court, Judge Guy Whitburn gave the burglar seven years and Terry £100 for 'public-spirited action'. The judge told Terry, 'I only wish you'd hit him harder.'

Sun

In a court case involving Jaffa Cakes the defence proved that when stale a biscuit goes soft and a cake goes hard. A Jaffa Cake goes hard and, therefore, is not a biscuit and not liable to VAT.

John E. Foster, head of Catering and Conference Services, Imperial College London, *The Times*

Richard Littlejohn had a go at Scotland Yard chief Ian Blair for asking all his officers if they were homosexual. 'Why?' he asked. 'Most of us couldn't care less. We want them pounding the beat in pairs, even if it does mean them holding hands.'

Daily Mail

A 42-year-old man found guilty of stealing women's underwear received an ASBO banning him from the Isles of Scilly for seven years.

Western Morning News

Compensation Culture:

Prisoners in Scottish jails sue over the degradation of slopping out.

Prison officers sue over the degradation of watching prisoners slop out.

The Times

A man from Eccles, Greater Manchester, who netted more than £17,000 in disability payments, got a six-month jail sentence after social security investigators discovered that he had medals and trophies charting his rise to a black belt in ju-jitsu. They also found photographs of him riding a camel in Tunisia and wrestling an alligator in Florida.

Reader's Digest

Stephen Sinnott, 49, who claimed nearly £23,000 on the grounds that he could barely walk, was exposed as an accomplished half-marathon runner.

Acting on a tip-off, government inspectors filmed him on a training run from a Liverpool leisure centre. Afterwards, he was seen jogging to where he had parked his Motability car.

Daily Telegraph

Henley Standard columnist Thomas Octavius recalls some boisterous roisterers at the town's Royal Regatta back in the 50s. A rowing crew with a reputation for mayhem hired a barge and the local police thought it wise to have a bobby keep an eye on them. The crew invited the PC on board for a drink and hours later they carried a comatose constable back to the station, saying, 'This one doesn't work. Can we have another?'

A woman who complained about a taxi driver urinating against his cab was told that he was doing nothing wrong. A 158-year-old law states that hackney carriage drivers may urinate against the rear offside wheel.

The Times

In May 2005, the *Sun* published a list of ancient laws that still exist:

- London cabbies should ask passengers if they have small pox or plague.
- It is still OK to shoot a Welshman with a longbow in Hereford's Cathedral Close – but only on Sundays.
- It is legal to use a bow and arrow on a Scot in York – except on Sundays.
- A law still exists to stop people beating or shaking a carpet in any street in the Metropolitan Police District.

Sun

A 1997 report reminded us that it is still technically illegal to shout 'Taxi' to hail a cab. *Focus* magazine reported that it was apparently still unlawful for the police and other emergency services to work on Christmas Day. Even more oddly, serving more than three courses for Christmas dinner breaches an ancient law. And another one made it illegal to beat your wife after 9pm – because of the noise.

And it was against the law to make love on the steps of a church after sundown. *Focus* editor Paul Colbert said, 'I suppose it's allowed in broad daylight, is it?'

Independent

Consultant forensic physician Robert M. Bruce-Chwatt wrote to *The Times* about the case of a Nigerian arrested for fraud while carrying a forged South African passport. 'He cheerfully told me that he had already been deported from this country five times... and had no doubts that after his sixth deportation he would be back again.'

The Times

A burglar broke into a café on Swindon railway station, drank several cans of lager and then got stuck trying to escape through a window. He had to call for police help and was later fined £420.

The Times

Many prisoners prefer life inside because they are relieved of the anxiety of fending for themselves. They are fed, clothed and warm. Life is predictable and there is much less violence than on an average housing estate. It is easier to see a doctor in prison.

Theodore Dalrymple, *The Times*

Stephen Gough walked naked from Land's End to John O'Groats in 2003 and was arrested fourteen times and spent five months in jail. When he announced plans to do it again in 2005, the *Independent* asked, 'What does your mother think of it all?'

'I have a feeling that she is secretly quite proud,'

he replied. 'She gave me a statue of a naked man for Christmas last year.'

Independent

The Independent reported a crime which it described as 'a minor catastrophe of the sort you couldn't make up'. A performance of *The Knot Garden* at the Royal Opera House was held up after a contra-bassoon and two clarinets were pinched from the orchestra pit. The police turned up and caught the thieves trying to sell the instruments in Covent Garden, just around the corner.

'They weren't hard to spot,' said the ROH. 'The show went on after a slight delay.'

A thief awaiting sentence at Lewes magistrates' court got fed up of waiting, nipped outside and stole from a nearby store. The 25-year-old came running back minutes later – pursued by police officers, who arrested him.

The Times

Wine-shop manager Andy Smith spotted a thief grab a customer's purse and run off in Welwyn Garden City. The thief had the nerve to return to the shop two weeks later. Five police officers were outside in the street only yards away and Andy ran out to alert them. But the officers told him they couldn't help because they were busy putting out traffic cones.

Sun

A Dorset solicitor stole more than £825,000 from the Inland Revenue by paying money into a bogus bank account he set up in the name of 'Ian Revue'. He was jailed for three years and nine months at Bournemouth Crown Court.

Daily Telegraph

A bottle of melted ice from the Antarctic was exhibited at Dartington Hall, South Devon. It disappeared and police were called in to investigate whether a thirsty visitor had drunk what was designed as a sculptural reminder of the hazards of global warming.

Guardian

A BBC producer who cycles to work has calculated how much it would cost him in fines if he was prosecuted for every offence he committed on the way. On a typical journey to work he observed himself committing eleven separate offences – including going the wrong way along a one-way street, jumping red lights and riding in a non-cycling area of a Royal Park. With 160 journeys a year and a standard £30 fine per offence, the bill came to £52,800.

Sunday Telegraph

A police community officer confessed to stealing from the tea and biscuit fund at Pitsea police station in Essex.

News of the World

10-year-old Amy Osborn, of Ramsgate, Kent, was distraught when her toy tiger Tyrone fell out of the family car on the M11 – so police set up a roadblock to enable her cuddly stuffed pet to be retrieved. PC Al Cuthbertson scoured a nine-mile stretch of the motorway and found Tyrone on the central reservation between Stansted and Harlow, Essex.

An Essex police spokesman said that PC Cuthbertson had children of his own 'and knew the importance'.

Amy said, 'I think the police are brilliant.'

The Times/Daily Telegraph

Detective Chief Superintendent Jack Slipper ('Slipper of the Yard') died in August 2005. The distinguished detective was famous for tracking down Great Train Robber Ronnie Biggs in Brazil (with the considerable help of the *Daily Express*).

Keith Waterhouse describes Slipper as the archetypal copper 'from his neat moustache to his size-12 feet. He looked like a copper and talked like a copper. "Long time no see, Ronnie," he said, as he walked into Biggs's hotel room in Rio after a nine-year search. No cops and robbers screenwriter would have dared pen such a corny line. But Slipper was proud of it. He'd rehearsed it. He was a copper's copper.'

Daily Mail

The *Guardian* recalled the day when Slipper introduced himself to another Great Train Robber (Buster Edwards) in his customary manner: 'I'm Slipper of the Yard.'

'Is that slipper as in foot?' one of Buster's companions asked.

'That's right,' replied the detective. 'Slipper as in foot – right up your f**king arse.'

A proper copper, said the *Guardian*.

'Follow that barrow,' said police when farmer Chris Lees reported that a burglar had raided his farm at Nadderwater, Devon, and escaped – pushing his loot in a stolen barrow. Chris leaped into his Landrover and slowly tailed the thief along country lanes for five miles before the police turned up.

Jethro Smith, 23, got a two-year supervision order at Exeter Crown Court and a headline in *The Times*: 'Wheelbarrow thief caught in 2mph chase.'

Mick Ridley, 49, of Forthampton, near Tewkesbury, Gloucestershire, leaped from his bath and drove naked for two miles to catch up with a thief who had stolen his horse box. 'He looked at me with real shock,' said Mark. 'I don't think he was expecting to see a naked man after him.' Police arrested a shocked suspect.

The Times

Thieves stole 600 new Portsmouth Football Club strips. Fans bought them illegally from touts at half the official price of £40. At the next Portsmouth game, police swooped on stupid fans wearing the new strips before they had been released on the legitimate market.

Daily Telegraph

James and Mavis Coombes set up a night-vision camera to film the wildlife in their garden near Exeter. Foxes and badgers (one called Lulu) are regular visitors, but one night their camera revealed three burglars on their way to break into a neighbour's house. Police recognised one of them as an old customer of theirs, and at Exeter Crown Court he got four years. Said Mrs Coombes, 'We were glad to help the police, but we would rather stick to watching badgers and foxes in the future.'

Daily Telegraph/Daily Mail

In October 2005, it was reported that North Suffolk was deploying cardboard police officers. This prompted a letter from Les Wray of Thirsk, North Yorkshire, saying, 'Our local supermarket had one several years ago. He disappeared, presumably stolen.'

Daily Telegraph

A court was told that a woman plotted to smuggle nearly 600 Eastern European women into Britain in one of the largest cases of its kind.

Spotted by Margaret Garbutt, of Goodmayes, Essex, *BBC/Teletext*

Sue Cruickshank's Yorkshire terrier cross, Gemma, was run over and killed by a hit-and-run 4x4 in Shoreham, West Sussex. Mrs Cruickshank was refused access to CCTV footage that captured the incident – on the grounds that it would infringe the driver's rights under the Data Protection Act.

Daily Telegraph

Burglar David Gardner, 31, of Newcastle, once had to be rescued after getting stuck in a chimney when breaking into a pub. Later, when he was wanted for breaching his bail, he went on the run. He was caught visiting a friend in prison at Startforth, Co. Durham.

Daily Telegraph

Gentleman hero David Dalton was appalled at the rudeness of a bank robber who, when demanding money from a female clerk, snapped, 'I want it and I want it now.' He chastised the robber for his bad manners and held him until the police arrived.

Mr Dalton, a hospital computer analyst, said he couldn't abide bad manners and it was partly because the

young robber was so loutish and uncivil that he decided
to have a go. He got a bravery award from Brighton &
Hove Police and the loutish robber got five years.

Brighton Argus

An eleven-day anti-crime operation by Central
Scotland Police involved CID officers, a tactical
crime and drugs unit and operational staff. Among
the operation's successes was the discovery of an
'Aladdin's Cave' of stolen garden ornaments
including gnomes, birds, rabbits, frogs, hedgehogs
and a decorative wheelbarrow. 'A significant
achievement,' said a police spokesman.

Guardian

After being mugged twice, Harold Newton, a 70-year-old
market trader from Northwich, Cheshire, stuffed his
wallet with homemade £20 notes, which he intended to
hand over to any future muggers. They were crude
affairs. On the front, they were green, not purple and red
like the real thing. On the reverse, instead of a portrait
of Elgar and a view of Worcester Cathedral, they were
blank except for the word 'Gotcha'. Nevertheless, Harold
was hauled before Vale Royal Magistrates in Cheshire,
given a conditional discharge and order to pay £20 costs
– 'preferably in real money'.

The Times

Criminals impersonating staff at the Department of Work and Pensions stole some £30 million. The Ephraim Hardcastle column says it is informed that the enterprising fraudsters appropriated the identities of members of the Department's fraud squad.

Daily Mail

Ted Reynolds of Southsea, Hampshire, tells of the time when he was a prison officer in charge of a prisoner at the Old Bailey. The judge passed down a sentence of fifteen years and the prisoner shouted, 'But I am an old man, I'll never see it out!'

'Do the best you can,' said the judge.

Daily Mail

Essex Police vehicles were caught on speed cameras more than 5,000 times in the first six months of 2005. During that time, there are no recorded cases of Essex officers being disciplined for speeding offences.

BBC News

A contract is a contract, even if it is a contract to kill. Kevin Reeves, 40, was jailed for fifteen months at Maidstone Crown Court after accepting £20,000 from a depressed friend who asked him to find a hitman to murder her. Reeves offered to do it himself, but got no further than pocketing the money. The intended victim, clearly annoyed at being still alive, filed a complaint for breach of contract. The prosecution conceded that the case was bizarre and the defence conceded, 'This is a wholly unattractive case.'

The Times

Only one crime in every hundred results in an offender being caught and punished in the courts. There were 32.7 million crimes in England and Wales in the year to March 2005. Only 317,000 criminals were sentenced.

Daily Mail

A dossier of more than 500 emails from regular policemen contains complaints about some civilian community support officers (CSOs) being lazy and incompetent. The dossier was compiled by the Metropolitan Police Federation and includes allegations of CSOs brawling with each other in the streets, urinating in public and eating and shopping while supposedly on patrol.

Daily Mail

The Law Commission's Statute Law Revision team are kept busy sifting through ancient laws which are still valid. In January 2006, it reported that it was still unlawful:

- To beat or shake your doormat outside after 8am.

- To visit the Houses of Parliament wearing a suit of armour.
- To be drunk in charge of a cow or a steam engine.
- To slide on snow or ice, or fly a kite.
- To hang washing across the street.
- To keep or use, or act in the management of any house, room, pit or other place for the purpose of fighting or baiting lions, bears or other animals.
- To wilfully and wantonly disturb residents by ringing their doorbells.
- If you should find a dead whale, remember that the head belongs to the King and the tail belongs to the Queen, who may need its bones for her corsets.

The Times/Daily Mail

Giving a policeman (or woman) a kiss on New Year's Eve has long been popular among high-spirited revellers. But as New Year's Eve approached during 2005 the Metropolitan Police ruled that kissing a PC is no longer PC and officers were told, 'Amorous persons are to be kept at arm's length.'

Sunday Telegraph

Freed jailbird Martin Kilpatrick wanted to go back inside so he robbed a bookies and then went up to a policeman and said, 'I've just done Coral's.' Durham Crown Court obliged with a sentence of three and a half years.

Sun

Under the headline 'Compensation Culture', *The Times* printed a list of cases that included:
- Lorraine Capener, mortuary technician, received £15,000 compensation after developing a morbid fear of death.
- A Scottish police officer got £2,000 after being bitten by his own dog.
- A British soldier got £75,000 from the MOD. He fell from an army lorry as he 'windsurfed' on the tailgate.
- Convict Karl Jones got nearly £248,000 after claiming erectile dysfunction after slipping into an uncovered drain in a shower in a Norfolk jail.

The Times

Police came up with a novel new way to be tough on crime at a troubled housing estate in Norwich. They advised residents to spray Jeyes Fluid in the stairwells of their flats in the hope that the pungent odour would stop gangs of youths, drunks and prostitutes gathering there.

Said a triumphant neighbourhood police officer, 'It worked.'

Daily Telegraph

Craig Conn, 21, whooped with delight and punched the air when he was released on bail for four weeks to await sentencing for assault. His behaviour so infuriated Sheriff Robert Dickson, sitting in Airdrie court in Lanarkshire, that he had Conn handcuffed and told him he would now be going to jail while awaiting background reports. Said Sheriff Dickson, 'You won't be going whoopee in this court. While we wait for the report you will be held in custody.'

The Times/Telegraph

It seemed like a bright idea, equipping the police officers who patrol London's parks with roller blades. But the scheme to speed up the bobbies collapsed, as did some of the officers, when villains quickly discovered that cops on skates could not pursue them over grass. The law enforcers reverted to old technology – bikes.

The Times

A man was charged with possessing controlled substances following a joint operation between uniformed and CID officers.

Oban Times/Guardian

Chapter 5

Media Madness

**Fleet Street lives on. The office of
<u>The Beano</u> is still there...**

In his *Daily Telegraph* diary, Jeremy Paxman
revealed how someone had called him a racist c**t
and Paxo replied, 'And they say Socratic dialogue
is dead'.

'Actually,' the man replied, 'Socrates thinks you
are a c**t as well!'

Stories about the inventive skills of journalists when
writing their expenses are legend. The *Press Gazette*
tells the one about the racing correspondent, a father of
four, whose expenses were challenged because a
restaurant bill included 'Children's Meals x 4'.

'I was entertaining jockeys,' explained the correspondent.

The column in which the *Guardian* corrects its mistakes is described by Keith Waterhouse as the funniest feature in journalism. Examples:

- We spelled Morecambe, the town in Lancashire, wrong again yesterday. We often do.
- The judge said to have admitted falling asleep during a trial may have been somnolent. He certainly wasn't somnambulant. Somnolent: drowsy, sleepy; somnambulant: walking while asleep.
- We spoiled the punchline in the joke used to trail the C4 programme on the history of Jewish comedy. We told it like this: 'What's the difference between a rottweiler and a Jewish mother? A Jewish mother will eventually let go...' The punchline should read: 'A rottweiler will eventually let go.'
- The absence of corrections yesterday was due to a technical hitch rather than any sudden onset of accuracy.

From *Only Correct*: *The Best of Corrections and Clarifications* by Ian Mayes, readers' editor of the *Guardian*

'NOTHING STOLEN'

The nearside front window of a Renault Clio car in Oxford Road, Halstead, was smashed but nothing was stolen. The *Press Gazette* reproduced this report with the caption: 'A rip-roaring story from the *Colchester Evening Gazette*, sold with such panache by the headline.'

A slight hiccup at the *Spectator* magazine after it installed a swear box. 'Somebody's nicked the bloody thing,' writes Stuart Reid, acting editor, writing in the *Catholic Herald*.

Sam Leith, literary editor of the *Daily Telegraph*, writes in the *Press Gazette* about one of his first editors (Rory Knight-Bruce, then running the *Evening Standard*'s Londoner's Diary). The young Sam pointed out a grammatical error to Rory, who responded with: 'Look, Leith, if you want to be an academic, f*ck off to Oxford! If you want to be a journalist, shut up and do what I say!'

Later, young Sam asked if he could have a rise and Rory replied, 'Nope. But you must never be afraid to ask.'

The 'Dumb Britain' column, edited in *Private Eye* by Marcus Berkman, collects some of the most stupid answers to TV and radio quiz questions, and it is remarkable how many emanate from Anne Robinson's *The Weakest Link*. Some examples:

Q: In the City of London, the Monument commemorates which 17th-century event?
A: Err... the First World War?
Q: Which month in the Gregorian calendar is named after Augustus Caesar?
A: June.
Q: Single combat is a fight between how many people?
A: One person.
Q: In which city is the Scottish Parliament situated?
A: London.

In June 2005, there was a service in St Bride's, 'mother church of Fleet Street hacks', to mark the removal of the last news organisation (Reuters) from the Street of Adventure. Fleet Street was for many, many years the home of some of the best and worst newspapers in the world. But one revered publication still has an office in what has also been called the Street of Shame. It's *The Beano* comic – and *The Times* marked the occasion with the headline: 'Fleet Street is left to the Bash Street Kids as the press withdraws'.

Simon Hoggart tells this story about Brian Redhead, who used to be northern editor of the *Guardian* and 'a leading figure in Manchester journalism, never lacking in self-esteem'. Brian was having lunch with Alistair ('Letter from America') Cooke, then the *Guardian*'s US correspondent, when a waiter came over and said, 'If I tell my wife I heard that famous voice and didn't get an autograph, she would never forgive me.' Brian signed the waiter's book and handed it straight back.

Guardian

In an article on how Madonna now likes to live the life of an English lady, the *Daily Mail* reported that, according to *American Vogue*, she used to hate it when the British tabloids started calling her 'Madge'. Then a friend told her that it was short for 'Your Majesty' so she decided: 'OK, I like it.'

Daily Mail

Coronation Street celebrated its 45th anniversary in 2005 after winning a sackful of awards. The *Observer* magazine's cover story on Britain's favourite soap recalled a quote from the late Russell Harty: 'There was life before *Coronation Street* – but it wasn't up to much.'

When the *Daily Telegraph* became the only big-circulation national newspaper to keep its broadsheet format, readers rushed to praise it.

- One reader was overjoyed to have a newspaper still big enough to cover his car's windscreen to prevent frost.
- Another was pleased that it was a precise fit as a lining for the rabbit hutch.
- A charity shop said that 'only the broadsheet *Telegraph* will do when it comes to wrapping bric-a-brac'.
- Peter Mann, of East Hatley, Cambridgeshire, wrote, We took up the *Telegraph* after *The Times* 'switched to comic format'. It is perfect for muddy boots.

Daily Telegraph

When the *Guardian* changed from being a broadsheet to its new 'Berliner' size in 2005, the response was generally favourable. But you can't please all of the people all of the time. Sara Green, of Colchester, Essex, wrote to say that she loved the new size but objected to every page having colour. 'My wormery,' she wrote, 'needs a constant supply of shredded newspaper and colour print is poison to my worms. Could you use only black on both sides of one sheet of each paper?'

Guardian

Come the New Year a cocksure media devotes an unwarranted amount of time telling us what is going to happen in the next 365 days. Nick Cohen in the *Observer* indulges in debunking the practice with this personal illustration: 'I know a lot about politics and have only a passing interest in racing. But the odds are that I am more likely to get the winner of the Gold Cup right than foresee who will be in No. 10 next Christmas.'

Cohen recalls the study by Philip E. Tetlock in 'Expert Political Judgement', which reached the blunt conclusion that a chimpanzee throwing darts at a selection of answers pinned to a darts board was more likely to get it right than distinguished pundits.

Observer

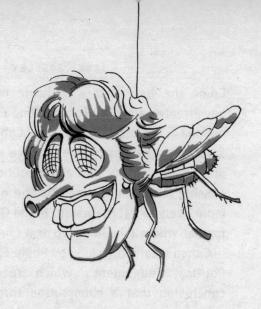

The Golden Camilla

Chapter 6

Royal Flush

**Prince Charles and Camilla call each
other Fred and Gladys...**

To make absolutely sure that no one would fail to recognise the VIP who was visiting a factory on the Isle of Sheppey, the VIP was provided with a name tag to wear on her overall. The tag revealed, in bold capital letters, that the visitor was, in fact, THE QUEEN.

Photograph in the *Sunday Telegraph*

When introduced to Barbara Windsor, the Queen greeted the busty star of *EastEnders* and many *Carry On* films with: 'You've got more clothes on today, haven't you?'

Sunday Telegraph

When Prince Charles and his sons William and Harry went hunting, Princess Diana used to call them 'the killer Wales'.

Independent on Sunday

Actor Sir John Mills ('impeccable English gentleman, a thread of tweed running through England') died in April 2005. He and his beloved wife Mary were inseparable. One night, at a grand dinner, they were seated apart and Sir John asked the waiter to pass a note to Mary – 'the attractive woman sitting opposite'. The waiter mistakenly delivered the note to Princess Diana and the message on it said, 'Do you fancy my place tonight? We could have some fun.'

Sunday Telegraph

Prince Charles paid £475 for a 'Victorian throne seat' for his lavatory. The makers said the extra large walnut seat 'is suitable for a very large rear'.

Sun

A new salmon angling fly has been created by the Atlantic Salmon Trust (of which Prince Charles is a patron). It is called the Golden Camilla and is modelled on the Duchess's thick mane of blonde hair. But some fishermen are worried that the hand-tied lure is frightening salmon away because it looks so ferocious.

The Times

The relationship between the Queen and Camilla continues to fascinate media commentators. Rebecca Tyrell writes, 'Happily, the two women are physically quite similar; chesty, short-legged, and have enough mutual interests: pruning, dogs and socially inadequate men.'

Sunday Telegraph

When Camilla ordered some shoes to be made and sent on from a sewing workshop in the oasis town of Siwa, she was asked for her home address. A wag replied, 'A rather large palace in the centre of London.'

Daily Mail

A *Daily Telegraph* writer was moved to comment on 'an extraordinary' newspaper picture of the Queen and film director Michael Winner at a damp ceremony in the Mall. 'He holds an umbrella above his head. The Queen is without cover. Shades of Raleigh!'

Later, Michael Winner said he had been asked by the Queen to hold her umbrella while she laid a wreath.

Daily Telegraph

When Prince Charles visited a school in Scotland, he noticed they had put tarmac down over a large area and he said, 'Why can't you dig up some of it and allow the children to grow vegetables?'

Later, the school revealed that the tarmac had been laid for safety reasons for his visit.

BBC/News of the World

'I keep a thermos flask full of champagne. It's one of my little treats.' The late Queen Mother, quoted in *Wrinkles, Wit & Wisdom* by Rosemary Jarski, published by Prion.

Daily Mail

Shortly before the Queen's 80th birthday party on 21 April 2006, the *Daily Mail's* Ephraim Hardcastle column wondered how it would compare with her mother's 80th celebrations in 1980. On that occasion, the Queen Mother 'roped in high-spirited guests for a convivial luncheon party at which extra-strong dry martinis were served'. An elderly peer mixing the martinis was instructed by the Queen Mum, 'Don't stint on the gin!'

Daily Mail

The Prince of Wales breakfasts off wheatgerm, lunches off dry bread and dines like the Emperor Nero... His grandfather used to kick furniture so hard that his hosts hid their antiques when he came to stay... A former servant claims that Charles wrenched a hand basin from the wall and wrote terse notes to staff such as: 'This sponge is dry. Please see that it is watered immediately'... Camilla is a jolly Gloucestershire matron with a voice that could trigger a Klosters avalanche.

From a page-long profile in the *Observer*

Among the Gloucestershire set, Camilla is known as 'a bit of all right' – earthy, fun and just what the doctor ordered.

Observer

Bottled water with Prince Charles's organic label on it is on sale at four times the price of water that cannot boast the Duchy Originals brand, even though both come from the same Highland well.

Observer

The Queen was crowned top frown in a poll to find the world's most miserable celebrity. Anne Robinson grimaced her way into second place. The poll of unsmiling celebs was organised by a firm which makes a teeth-whitening system.

Sun

Along with his fellow recruits at Sandhurst, Prince Harry is to be given lessons in how to behave at table – including which cutlery to use and how to give the Loyal Toast. He will be taught:

- To talk to the person on his left during the first course, followed by the person to his right for the main course.
- Not to leave the table to visit the lavatory until the end of the Loyal Toast.
- That port is always served by the host, who will pour a glass for the person on his right – and then himself before passing the bottle round the table to the left. In some regiments, the decanter is not allowed to touch the table. Others insist it never leaves the table.

Daily Mail

A former Sandhurst cadet admitted that 'given his upbringing' Prince Harry should have a good start on how to behave – but he warned, 'Sometimes cadet pranksters will tie your chair leg to the table to prevent you from standing during the toasts.'

Daily Mail

In their private correspondence, Prince Charles and Camilla used to refer to each other as Fred and Gladys. The nicknames never seemed more appropriate than when they toured the Middle East in March 2006 dressed like a no-longer-young couple taking the air in Eastbourne or Cleethorpes.

Daily Mail

They're a hungry lot – the people who get invited to the Queen's garden parties. So much so that the company doing the catering ended up running at a loss. On average, each of those attending ate fourteen cakes, sandwiches and ice creams. One royal aide said wryly, 'They certainly got good value for the 61p a year it costs them for the monarchy.'

Daily Telegraph

In 2004, the Queen entertained 39,000 guests to six garden parties on the lawns of Buckingham Palace and Holyroodhouse in Edinburgh. Total cost: £500,000.

Daily Telegraph

News that Charles and Camilla were planning a visit to New York got a whiskery old joke going the rounds in Manhattan. An old lady, alone with her cat, is polishing a lamp when a genie appears and offers two wishes. The old lady asks to be made young again and for the cat to become a prince. The genie does his stuff and the prince whispers: 'Now aren't you sorry you had me neutered?'

Ephraim Hardcastle, *Daily Mail*

The Ministry of Defence raised some eyebrows when it proposed to 'hire out' the Queen at a party to mark the bicentenary of the Battle of Trafalgar. The Guardian reported that 'members of the public will, it seems, be able to pay £1,750 to meet Her Majesty'.

As a cheaper alternative, the newspaper said the Queensbridge Community Centre in East London could be hired for £60 an hour. 'You get the use of the sports hall and they'll throw in a bouncy castle.'

Guardian

Prince Harry stopped off at a McDonald's in Plymouth, ordered a chicken burger and a strawberry milkshake – and sat outside on the pavement, tucking in. McDonald's said, 'We are delighted that the prince decided to take part in our "Buy One and Get One Free" offer.'

Western Morning News

Henry VIII granted Lord Forester the right to keep his hat on in the presence of the Sovereign. Forester was told that he should 'wear his bonnet at all times owing to certain infirmities of the heade'. This right was granted in perpetuity and, reputedly, a later Lord Forester was emboldened to keep his hat on in the presence of Queen Victoria. She was not amused and, when informed of the Royal Warrant, made the acerbic reply: 'In the presence of the monarch maybe; in the presence of a lady, never.'

Lady Forester, of Broseley, Shropshire, writes in the *Daily Telegraph* of 26 September 2005: 'On that premise, my husband was never tempted to exercise his right.'

Since Harold's defeat at Hastings, we English have not been ruled by a wholly English sovereign.

Canon Robert Baily, Grantham, Lincs,
Daily Telegraph

When US TV cameras were allowed into Windsor Castle in October 2005, *The Times* remarked on the show's 'awe and reverence' during the visit to 'Her Majesty's most gracious home'. ABC's *Good Morning America* programme indulged America's enduring Anglophilia, and the majesty of Her Majesty's Thameside castle was described as being, well, 'majestic'.

There was no danger of the cameras catching a glimpse of the Queen. She was being majestic hundreds of miles away from the cameras – amid the majesty of another of her majestic homes – in Balmoral, Scotland.

The Times

The *Daily Telegraph* said the ABC show gave Americans the sort of coverage that the Royal Family would kill for in Britain... 'bathing the monarchy in soft soap'.

Daily Telegraph

The late Queen Mother was well known for her love of gin and Dubonnet. But Hugo Vickers' new biography, Elizabeth, The Queen Mother, reveals that she was so fond of chocolates that she sometimes even ate the Good Boy dog chocs kept for her corgis.

Sun

The Queen Mother was a 'Mad Hatter' – one of a group of aristocratic young ladies who burst on to the social scene after World War I. One or two in this set were considered fast, notably her friend Mollie Lascelles, dubbed 'Midnight Mollie'. She was what the 10th Duke of Marlborough described as 'a kind girl', the sort who went further than their more cautious contemporaries.

An excerpt from Hugo Vickers' biography published by Hutchinson, *Daily Mail*

Who would blame the Queen if she heaved a sigh of relief when the President of China's State Visit was over in November 2005? The Chinese left most of their food on their plates. President Hu Jintao demanded that his drinking glasses be sterilised and insisted that his bedroom suite in Buckingham Palace was completely blacked out. Furniture made of light wood had to be exchanged for dark. And at the stately banquet one of the Chinese entourage tapped away at his laptop between courses.

Sun

There was much upset over the mergers of famous British Army regiments in 2005. Prince Charles reported difficulty in keeping up with all the changes and complained that his ceremonial uniforms were sometimes out of date before he'd had a chance to wear them.

Daily Telegraph

Rolf Harris was commissioned by the BBC to paint a portrait of the Queen to celebrate her 80th birthday. Some art critics were sniffy about this, but *The Times* critic Rachel Campbell-Johnson said his picture was perfectly competent – 'an affectionate portrait capturing the Queen sitting like many an old lady by the window of her front room. She might have been watching the neighbours through the nets.'

The Times

The Queen and the Duke of Edinburgh were visiting an RAF station and an 8-year-old girl presented Her Majesty with a bouquet. The Duke asked the little girl, 'Did you grow these yourself?'

She replied, 'Of course not, silly.'

Mrs Marjorie Ross, Bournemouth, *Daily Mail*

A proud moment for the England women's cricket team – an invitation to Buckingham Palace to celebrate victory in their version of the Ashes. Prince Philip, who turned up in his private London taxi, examined the ladies' trophy and opined that it was a bit crumby and looked 'like a design and technology project gone wrong.'

Team captain Clare Connor said afterwards, 'We don't have an urn like the men. Ours is a cricket ball on a stand. We had a bit of a giggle and I told him he could design a new one.'

Daily Telegraph

The Queen's love for Prince Philip began to blossom in 1943 when she was 17. She wrote to a friend, 'I am now the proud possessor of a very large photograph of Philip, which stands on the mantelpiece and glowers at me. I had to go through a lot of ragging when it arrived, though Mummy said, "He is a good-looking boy," at which I agreed!'

Also in 1943, she met the dashing young naval officer at a weekend house party and wrote, 'We had a terrific time on Sunday night. We danced to the gramophone.'

The Times

When Charles visited the US with Diana, the Americans were dazzled by the young Princess. When he went there with Camilla in 2005, the *Miami Herald* described the visit as 'the Un-Diana tour... for a couple of middle-aged earnest eccentrics from the English countryside'.

Independent on Sunday

When arrangements were being made for the Queen to distribute Maundy Money at Guildford Cathedral in April 2006, the Palace was asked, 'What if her Majesty requires facilities?' implying that the Cathedral's might not be adequate for the Royal needs.

The Palace responded: 'Her Majesty NEVER requires facilities.'

Ephraim Hardcastle, *Daily Mail*

'Reasons given to the RSPCA by people abandoning their pets'

Chapter 7

Animal Magic

**Smoker gives up the habit –
for the sake of his two parrots...**

A Macaw called Barney, who used to belong to a truck driver, was given a private pen after telling visitors at the Warwickshire Animal Sanctuary – including the vicar and the mayor – to 'F*** off'.

Guardian

Noel Lightfoot, of Belton, South Yorkshire, tells of the day he was leaving Sheffield Wednesday's Hillsborough football ground when he heard a fan say to a mounted policewoman: "Ere, do you know your horse is foaming at the mouth?'

The policewoman replied, 'So would you be if you'd been between my legs for six hours.'

Daily Telegraph

A Liverpool pet shop complained that a dog was stealing the shop's dog biscuits. Police Officer William Kemp investigated – and found that the thieving canine belonged to him.

Dogs Today

Chris, of Headingley, Leeds, had a live-in girlfriend called Suzy and a parrot called Ziggy. Ziggy began to mimic Suzy, but when he did so, he squawked only one word: 'Gary'. Every time Suzy's mobile rang, Ziggy called out, 'Hi, Gary!'

One night Ziggy blurted out, 'I love you, Gary', and the Suzy-Chris relationship came to an end.

Unable to bear Ziggy's continuing references to Gary, Chris got rid of his beloved parrot and said, 'I'll get over Suzy, but I don't think I'll ever get over Ziggy. He never liked Suzy and she never took to him.'

Suzy said, 'I'm surprised he's got rid of that bloody bird. He spent more time talking to it than he did to me.'

Guardian

Stories of big, panther-like cats stalking the British countryside are a never-ending source of headlines. There was one reported to inhabit the area around the remote moorland village of East Ogwell in

Devon. However, the Beast of Ogwell turned out to be Sebastian – the pet of Mike Healey – weighing in at two stone and one of the fattest domestic pussies in Britain. Said owner Mike, 'The only time he is a danger is when he lies on you.'

The Times

Buster, a South Yorkshire police dog, got the boot after an official report condemned him for having 'a wilful good nature'. The Alsatian never barked and encouraged rowdy drunks to stroke him.

Yorkshire Post/The Times

Derbyshire police dogs have been tested to make sure their barks do not break noise pollution regulations.

Daily Telegraph/BBC News

Brian Swindles and Sarah Oakley of Blyth Bridge, Staffordshire, wanted to adopt a stray puppy from their local animal shelter. They were stunned to be told they could not have one because they were not married. Said Brian, a 22-year-old mechanical engineer, 'It's ridiculous. We could adopt a child, but not a dog.'

Daily Mail

Police launched a hunt for vandals after £200,000 worth of new-registration vehicles parked in a field at Haverfordwest had their doors and sides bashed in. Later, it emerged that the vandal was an angry ram, which had been butting its reflection in the shiny bodywork.

The Times

In Newbury, several plastic owls and falcons have been placed on rooftops to scare pigeons away. Patrick Painting, of Newbury, tells how he often sees pigeons sitting on the heads of an eagle owl and other raptors – totally unconcerned.

Daily Telegraph

John Foot, of Highcliffe, Dorset, put a large plastic owl in a tree in his garden. Friends and neighbours, completely deceived, turned up with cameras and binoculars. Local wildlife remains oblivious – and the pigeons multiply.

Daily Telegraph

Top TV programmes among Britain's pampered pets are snooker, *Coronation Street*, *EastEnders* and *Animal Hospital*.

Sun and Marks & Spencer
insurance researchers

London mayor Ken Livingstone famously described pigeons as 'flying rats'. But up North the passion for racing pigeons is deeply engrained. Stephen Elliott's wife asked him, 'What would you do if you had the chance, pack the pigeons in, or pack me in?'

The Northumbrian pigeon fancier replied, 'Don't ask the question.'

Stephen says one of his friends has 'pigeon racing' cited in his divorce papers.

Guardian

Sad news for all lovers of PG Wodehouse, Lord Emsworth and his prize-winning Berkshire pig the Empress of Blandings. Wodehouse described the Empress as looking like 'a captive balloon... as nearly circular as a pig can be without bursting'.

An official of the Berkshire Pig Breeders Club has told *The Times*: 'We wouldn't want them quite as fat as that these days... If you wheeled the Empress into the show ring now she would probably be regarded as too fat. Fat is just not fashionable.'

The Times

A fox got the shock of its life after breaking into a hen coop at Shepton Mallet, Somerset. He got beaten 'to within an inch of his life' by a cockerel standing guard over five hens. Brer Fox was not to know that not only was the cockerel one of the biggest in Britain (35in tall and weighing 25lb) but was named Rooster Cogburn after John Wayne's sheriff character in *True Grit*. Cogburn's owner Tim Stone said that the coop ended up 'covered in blood and red fur'.

The Times

'The English take the breeding of their horses and dogs more seriously than they do their children. God forbid that the wrong drop of blood should get into their Labrador. But their children marry everywhere.'

Princess Michael of Kent quoted in a German newspaper, *Guardian*

The Scottish island of Canna is home to sixteen people – and about 10,000 rats. There is a project to exterminate the rats, but not until a colony of woodmice have been captured and taken to the safety of Edinburgh Zoo. Once the rats have been seen off, the mice will be returned to the island.

The Times

Something else to worry about. Street lamps and security lights could be leading to the extinction of glow worms. The UK Glow Worm Group says the worms are finding it hard to mate – males cannot see the glow given out by females because of light pollution.

Guardian

Labrador saves rabbit from drowning.

Paul Marshall was taking his Lab, Chester, for a walk near Richmond, North Yorkshire, when the dog flushed out a rabbit, which ran into a pond. Chester followed and the rabbit climbed on to the dog's back. Chester then carried his passenger to the bank and the rabbit escaped unharmed.

Daily Telegraph

Heavy smoker Mark Hutchinson, 41, of Newport, has given up after being told his two parrots were suffering from passive smoking.

Sunday People

Who's a silly boy then? When David Carlile burgled the Berkshire home of Diana Winter, widow of racing legend Fred Winter, he took the family's pet parrot. He did so because he believed that Monty, an African Grey, would be able to describe him to the police. Carlile didn't know that parrots only mimic words they already know and that Monty's vocabulary didn't go much beyond 'Hello, Darling'. Police collared Carlile without any help from Monty and he ended up in jail.

Daily Express

A UK-wide survey by the Royal Horticultural Society and the Wildlife Trusts found that the nation's favourite wild animal is the hedgehog. *The Independent* reported this joyous news along with a story that in the Royal Botanic Gardens at Kew there are 300 acres of territory perfect for hedgehogs. But there are none – because badgers have eaten every last one.

Independent

Keela, a 16-month-old South Yorkshire Police sniffer dog earns around £200,000 a year – more than Chief Constable Meredydd Hughes (£129,630). Keela is hired out at £530 a day (plus expenses), it was reported in 2005. She can detect minute quantities of blood that cannot be seen with the human eye and can sniff out blood in clothes after they have been washed repeatedly in biological washing powder.

The Times

Somebody complained to the local council about the early morning crowing of Nev Earnshaw's cockerels, Albert and Norman. Mr Earnshaw lives in Earswick village, near York, and among the responses he received from officialdom was the advice: 'Put socks over their heads'.

Daily Telegraph

As thousands of well-bred dogs descended on Birmingham for the 2006 Crufts dog show, *Country Life* magazine jumped head first into controversy with a mischievous survey of Best Breeds.

- MOST INTELLIGENT – the Bassett Hound – although 'it will find fetching your slippers a tough mental workout'.
- MOST PRACTICAL – the Pug. 'Every hotelier's favourite client, happily snoozing softly in the lap of a lady who lunches.'
- LEAST SOCIALLY ACCEPTABLE – the Bichon Frise. 'Quite ghastly... a teeth-gratingly pretentious name... powder-puff ears... feeble goatee beard... white toenails... makes the most coiffured Parisian poodle look rugged.'

Daily Mail

While David Hunt, 43, and his wife Nicola, 30, of Macclesfield, were on honeymoon in 2002, their mongrel bitch Holly went to stay with Nicola's parents 300 miles away in Liskeard, Cornwall. The parents had to go away for a few days and put Holly into nearby kennels. Holly escaped and the Hunts spent many weekends on 600-mile round trips from Macclesfield to Liskeard searching for Holly. When this failed, they moved from the North of England to live in Cornwall – allowing more searching time.

In 2006, four years after disappearing, Holly walked into a house only a few miles from the Liskeard kennels – 'absolutely filthy but in good condition'. Said a delighted Mr Hunt, 'She came up to me as if she'd been gone for a day – wagging her tail and licking me all over.'

Daily Express

Chapter 8

Food For Thought

The sausage roll made the British what we are...

Margaret Thatcher's relationship with her ministers was summed up in a sketch showing them all in a restaurant. She orders steak and the waiter asks, 'And what about the vegetables?'

'They'll have the same as me,' replies the Prime Minister.

Sun

Matt Bridgman's sister offered a friend's 3-year-old a biscuit and asked, 'What do you say?'
The child took hold of the biscuit and said, 'Let go.'
Matt Bridgman, Hertfordshire. *Daily Mail*

A *Times* reader tells about wining and dining a couple of old friends for a weekend. The couple arrived empty-handed, but a few days later the husband turned up to say thanks and gave them a small pot of homemade jam. The reader asks, 'Should I have called him a cheapskate or apologised for the thick skin of green mould that had grown on the jam in the six years since I had made and given it to them?'

Philip Howard replies, 'What better to get a wry smile out of the comedy of life, as you have.'

The Times

SHUN FAT is the name of a Chinese fish and chip shop in Bromyard, Herefordshire.

Spotted by Phil Iles of Hereford, *Daily Mail*

A lady from Swansea tells of a neighbour who was in a supermarket cafe ready to enjoy a cup of coffee and a Kit Kat. She ate one Kit Kat bar and then a stranger sharing her table leaned over and helped himself to a bar. The lady snapped off another bar and the man took the remaining bar. He then got up, went to the counter, bought another drink and a chocolate muffin and sat down at another table. Incensed, the lady got up to leave and, on her way out, grabbed the man's muffin, took a bite and put it back on his plate. She rushed out to her car, reached into her pocket for the car keys... and found a Kit Kat.

Daily Mail

Welsh cuisine has come a long way since the days of the following old recipe dug up by the 2005 edition of the *Cambria* magazine: Take a lump of bread, break it into a bowl, pour over hot water, then season with salt and pepper.

Ed Brooks, 29, ate 48ft of stinging nettles to win the 2005 World Nettle Eating Championship at the Bottle Inn, Marshwood, Dorset. His nearest rival was disqualified after 'a stomach evacuation incident'.

Sunday Times

Los Angeles-based *Times* writer Chris Ayres reports that the US Food and Drug Administration subjected a consignment of haggis to lab tests and reclassified the beloved Scottish dish as fertiliser. 'It is now on a list of forbidden imports, along with nerve gas and nuclear weapons.'

The Times

David Lilley, of Ashby de la Zouch, Leicestershire, writes to *The Times* about a bread and butter pudding he bought at a supermarket. It was labelled 'Perfect for Valentine's Day'. Lower down an information box said, 'Serves three'.

Simon Hopkinson's cookery book *Roast Chicken & Other Stories* was voted the most useful cookery book of all time in July 2005. But Dr Hilary Aitken, of Kilmacold, Inverness, challenged the chef's advice to 'Turn the oven off, leaving the door ajar, and leave the chicken to rest for at least fifteen minutes before carving.' Hopkinson, she said, 'has clearly never owned a cat.'

Daily Telegraph

This was followed by correspondence saying that any cat trying to raid Simon's oven would suffer severely singed whiskers, but Anthea Hanscomb, from Amersham, Buckinghamshire, chimed in with: 'I know a cat who, given half a chance, can hook a sausage from under the grill.'

Daily Telegraph

People think of it as being the simplest task in the kitchen – boiling an egg. But, when top chefs were asked for advice, they came back with five different answers.

- Michael Roux of the Waterside Inn, Bray, said: place the egg in a pan of cold water, bring to the boil, and then count to 60 seconds.
- Josh Emmett, Savoy Grill head chef, said: choose a small pan, bring water to a rolling boil, then gently lower the egg into the water. Boil for four and a half minutes.

- Giorgio Locatelli, chef-patron, Locanda Locatelli, London, said: boil the water first, add the egg and continue to boil for six minutes.
- Antonio Carluccio, cook and restaurateur, said: wash the egg, cook it in boiling water for three and a half minutes and leave to stand in the water for thirty seconds before serving.
- Delia Smith said: place the egg in cold water, bring it to the boil and cook for four minutes.

Guardian

Daily Telegraph reader Paul Chadwick, of Derby, said the top chefs failed to mention the most important point he learned from his granny: 'Once in the egg cup tap the top of the egg gently with a spoon. This prevents any further cooking.'

Guardian reader Jeremy Pitlove, of Leeds, said the only way is to put the egg into cold water, bring to the boil and then sing two verses of 'Now Thank We All Our God'.

In a long-running correspondence on sell-by dates, some contributors to *The Times* said that these dates 'could be safely ignored for a considerable time'. Neil P. Magee, of Edinburgh, told of a visit to a food-manufacturing plant where cottage cheese was being packed for three different leading retailers. One retailer had its tubs stamped with a sell-by date seven days later, the second ten days and the third fourteen days. Visitors were assured that the cheese would keep satisfactorily for at least four weeks.

The Times

A microbiologist from Cambridge expressed surprise at the early use-by dates on foods and wrote, 'Of course, the earlier the use-by date, the faster the turnover and consequently the greater the sales. Am I being unnecessarily suspicious?'

The Times

On the same day, a grandmother from Edinburgh told how she had served her grandchildren a stew from the freezer. Her 11-year-old grandson read the date on the freezer bag and said that the stew was older than he was.

The Times

After a report that a London restaurant was charging £108 for a bowl of shark's fin soup, the *Guardian* published a reader's claim that: 'Ironically, sharks' fins taste of nothing. The soup's flavour is provided by chicken stock.'

As the estimated cost of hosting the 2005 G8 Summit in Scotland spiralled towards £100,000,

The Times reminded the Scots that this sum would pay for 142,857,142 of one of the nation's favourite delicacies – deep-fried Mars Bars.

The sausage roll is an English peculiar declared a *Times*' leader. 'It is the ensemble of greasy puff pastry, grey mince stuffing, aromatic with pepper, sage and other spices, and faint intimations of neglected parts of pork that are at the heart of the matter... The sausage roll made the British what we are.'

To celebrate the centenary of the invention of the sausage roll, the *Sun* printed half a page of 'meaty facts about the classic British snack'.

- We invented them to insult the French. A Brit first shoved a sausage into a croissant to tease our Gallic neighbours about their breakfast pastry.
- By law, cooked sausage rolls must have a minimum of 12.5% meat. Uncooked, they must have 10.5%.
- On average, twenty-one tiny flakes of pastry are dropped with every bite.
- Georgina Sheron and David Herd, of Lancashire, met over a sausage roll at a petrol station. They plan to have a layered sausage roll wedding cake at their marriage ceremony.

In the midst of Jamie Oliver's campaign to improve school dinners, Joanna Moody, of Pateley Bridge, Yorkshire, remembered Thames Mud – 'a regular dish in the 1950s, consisting of lumpy chocolate custard with crumble that always seemed stony'.

Guardian

At Lou's Café at the Lambeth end of Westminster Bridge, the order for steak and kidney pudding with potatoes and cabbage used to be 'a baby's head and two'.

David Carle, Guildford, *Guardian*

In London's Docklands, 'baby's head twice' was a first course of a lump of suet with gravy, the second course was a lump of suet with custard.

Mark Jones of London, *Guardian*

The late father of Eleanor Jardine of Hertford taught in a convent in the 1970s when steamed suet roll was known as a nun's leg.

Guardian

Frances Ham of Blakemere, Herefordshire, remembers that at her convent school during the early 1960s steamed suet roll filled with bright red jam was not nun's leg, but, specifically, Reverend Mother's leg.

Guardian

Browsing the wine section of his local supermarket, Colin Munro, of Taunton, came across bottles to 'Serve with Red Meat', 'Serve with Chicken or Game', 'Serve with Pasta' and 'Serve with Friends'.

The Times

Derek Roberts, of Mitcham, Surrey, tells of his mother's 'very substantial Eccles cake' – known to the family as a fly cemetery.

Guardian

Rosemary Shewry, of St Albans, Hertfordshire, remembers her late mother-in-law producing strawberry-jam suet puddings rolled up in muslin and boiled in the washing 'copper'. They called it grandma's sore leg.

Guardian

Maggie Butcher, of London, writes that, when she was a child in North Buckinghamshire, a rolled-up boiled suet pudding with currants in was a bug in a bolster. Over the border, they put jam in one end and bacon and onions in the other and called it a Bedfordshire clanger.

Guardian

Cornish pasty fans in Fowey aim to beat the current record by devouring the county's favourite delicacy faster than anybody else. Devouring a 1lb pasty in less than 58 seconds is what is needed.

The town's August 2005 regatta was celebrated with a 6ft-long pasty.

Western Morning News

A fish and chip shop owner refused to serve traffic wardens after becoming fed up with them ticketing his customers in Waterfoot, Lancashire.

Sun

Baked beans are one of the most requested foods by the British on holiday abroad.

Sun

Breakfast at the Ritz costs £30. Further down Piccadilly at the Ponti café it costs £3.90.

Sun

They don't go for nouvelle cuisine much in Lancashire, but they do like a well-made pie, said the *Daily Telegraph*. Eight Burnley businessmen had one made with wagyu beef from Japan, matsutake mushrooms from Chinese Tibet, truffles, edible gold leaf, shallots, flour, eggs and fresh herbs. They washed it down with two bottles of 1982 Château Mouton Rothschild and two bottles of Louis Roederer Cristal Rose at a total cost of £8,195. They refused an offer of chips on the side because 'that would have been gilding the lily'.

Daily Telegraph

Restaurant critic Jan Muir tried out a new fad for 'ready-made gourmet meals delivered to your door'. Her verdict on some of the dishes delivered under the headline: 'Your dinner's in the post... and it tastes like a runner's shoe'.

- Boiled horse hoof.
- Fruit tart like a Frisbee of damp sponge with rabbit droppings.
- Beef stroganoff like two possums in the gutter – like road kill.
- Treacle tart like sugar-rich wallpaper paste.

Daily Telegraph

Arthur Boyt, 66, is a connoisseur of road-kill flesh and is writing a book of recipes which will include casseroles made from squashed badger, hedgehog, rabbit, otter and rat. For fifty years, he has regularly eaten animals run over near his home in Cornwall and has dined on squirrels, foxes, mice, deer and a great horseshoe bat. 'I've never been ill,' he says, adding that his favourite is badger sandwiches.

The Times (which printed Arthur's recipe for Hedgehog Spaghetti Carbonara)

Can man live on beer alone? *New Scientist* magazine readers have been asking such questions for years and now the answers have been compiled into a book. In fact, one pint will provide more than 5% of the daily recommended intake of vitamins B9, B6 and B2 – almost the same as a slice of brown bread. However, beer is low in vitamins A, C and D, and is a diuretic and will eventually leave you dehydrated.

Extracts from *Does Anything Eat Wasps?*
Edited by Mick O'Hare (Profile), *Daily Mail*

And, if you must know, wasps are a delicacy for many creatures such as birds, skunks, weasels, bats, rats – and even other wasps. Humans have also been known to fry them in butter...

Pernickety Prince Charles likes his sarnies in an organic bap precisely 8 cm wide, with pesto, mayonnaise, a fried egg cooked on both sides, two thin slices of Gruyère cheese – and don't forget the Marmite.

Daily Mail

Perhaps no surprise, then, that his mother once wrote: 'Charles is getting fatter. He has an endless appetite.' This was in 1950, when the Prince was nearly 2...

The *Observer Food Magazine (OFM)* checked out some posh London restaurants where it is nigh on impossible for ordinary people to get a table. When one of them said it was fully booked, the *OFM* said, 'It's for Mick Jagger.'

They were then told, 'That's fine. The boss would kill me if I said no.'

Pet food is often healthier than many fast foods, containing less fat, sugar and salt. Laboratory tests found one popular brand of cat meat contained 2.9g of fat per 100g – one-eighth the level of some chicken pieces and less than a third than that of some burgers and pizzas. 'It would not do a human any harm to eat this pet food. The taste would be a bit different from what you'd expect, but nutritionally it is fine,' said a scientist.

All pet food ingredients must be fit for human consumption according to EU law.

Sunday Times

Tripe has been voted Britain's most detested food – followed by jellied eels and deep-fried Mars bars.

BBC Olive magazine

A Morden, Surrey, grandmother asked her 3-year-old granddaughter if she would like some yoghurt.

'No,' said the girl.

'No, what?' asked the granny.

'No fear!' said the girl.

Daily Mail

'Melon selection'

Chapter 9

Sex – There's a Lot of It About!

Scandalised Victorians feared that bicycles would foster improper relations and provide sexual arousal...

A woman who passed out in an Asda supermarket was found to be wearing vibrating knickers. *Sun* columnist Richard Littlejohn chose this as his story of the week and commented, 'You couldn't make it up.'

Sunday Telegraph columnist Nigel Farndale wrote about sex education and told how his older sister talked him through the basics when he was about 7. He refused to believe her 'on the grounds that I couldn't imagine the Queen and Prince Philip doing anything so disgusting'.

The British Snoring and Sleep Apnoea Association said that lots of couples hardly ever had sex because their partner snored. Roger C. Bryan, of Bristol, suggested that things might improve if both parties were awake during lovemaking.

The Times

J. Procter of Greater Manchester wrote to the *Independent* that he was delighted to read that vigorous sex burns off 121 calories per hour. 'Please stand forward,' he said, 'all those who can manage the full hour.'

Marina Hyde's diary in the *Guardian* tells the story of the commuters who said nothing when a couple had sex on their train. But they objected most vociferously when the amorous pair lit post-coital cigarettes in the no-smoking carriage.

This story was current during the Cold War: Russia's Psychological Warfare unit asked the United States to supply one million condoms for the Red Army, specifying a length of ten inches. The US sent them along stamped 'Medium'.

Guardian

A visitor to a book-signing session for Tracey Cox's volume *Supersex* said that one of the positions illustrated 'doesn't look possible'. 'It is if you have a large penis,' she said, and her male questioner slunk away without a word.

Independent

A group of Oxford dons bathing naked in the Cherwell were surprised when a punt full of ladies floated by. Most of the red-faced dons covered their loins – except one who covered his head and later explained, 'I like to think that in Oxford I am recognised by my face.'

Letter in *The Times*

Bill Bryson told the Royal Geographical Society that he was once asked what he would like people to say about him in a hundred years' time. 'After a long think,' said the author, 'I came up with: "And the amazing thing is that he is still sexually active."'

The Times

In August 2002, the *Sun* reported that Madame Tussauds had to dry-clean the dress on Kylie Minogue's waxwork because tourists made it grubby by fondling her rear.

Sun

In May 2005, Tussauds had to make a new waxwork of Robbie Williams. The last one wore out because so many fans could not resist stroking it. *The Times* story was accompanied by a photograph of two shapely ladies kissing the new model and stroking its manly bare chest.

115

A think-tank report claims that the British have more sex than anyone else in Europe bar the French. The UK score 135 times a year, while the French manage 144. The British also have sex earlier than anyone else bar the Germans – UK average age is 17 years and one month. The Germans start at 16 years and nine months.

Daily Telegraph

In a survey of how long men take to make love, British males beat all their international rivals by taking longest to finish with 7 minutes 36 seconds. US males took 7.0 minutes and Spaniards were third at 5.8 minutes. Researchers said they set out to measure 'intravaginal ejaculation latency time'.

Journal of Sexual Medicine/
Independent on Sunday

A 200-year taboo was broken in May 2005 with the first public performance of bawdy songs by Robert Burns – songs he used to keep in a locked drawer because they were 'not for maids, ministers or striplings'. Under-18s were barred from Ayr Town Hall when folk musicians performed the songs. *The Times* published eight lines from one of them, but the average Sassenach would have difficulty in recognising anything naughty other than the bawdy bard's claim that 'Nine inch will please a lady'.

The Times

The Lordship of Purse Candle in North Dorset includes the historic right to bed the brides of servants on their wedding night.

Daily Telegraph

A woman who got fed up of a couple petting in a car outside her home in Linthorpe, Middlesbrough, cooled their passion by spraying her hosepipe through the car window.

Sun

People on the beach called 999 after hearing screams coming from a rubber dinghy bobbing in the sea off Paignton in Devon. Police and the coastguard and the lifeboat services raced to the scene – and found a naked couple making noisy love.

Sunday Times

A £60,000-a-year oil industry executive told a London industrial tribunal that he was sacked after spurning his female boss's offer of sex. He said that his boss invited him back to her place and said, 'I frequently wander around the house naked. I don't suppose that you will mind that – the old guy across the street doesn't seem to.'

The Times

The *Sunday Times* runs a weekly column called 'The Shock Exchange – The Tabloid Week'. In October 2005, it reported that the *Sun* was celebrating twenty-five years of advice from agony aunt Deirdre Sanders. Some of the problems that Deirdre has handled down the years were reproduced, including one about a girl who kept on calling her lover by the wrong name. The lover complained that he had lost count of the number of times she 'called me Tom, Dick or Harry – anything but my name, which is Derek. I still love her very much, but when I'm in her flat I get the feeling that someone has been there before.'

Sunday Times

Guides on sex and how to do it have been around since the days of the ancient Chinese, and the earliest known manuals go back to 300BC. The invention of the printing press enabled publishers to churn them out 'faster than the Church could ban them'.

In 1561, a volume by Mrs Isabella Cortes included the handy hint that a mixture of quails' testicles, large winged ants, musk and amber was perfect for straightening out bent penises.

In 1858, Dr William Acton wrote in 'Functions and Disorders of the Reproductive Organ' that: 'The majority of women (happily for them) are not very much troubled with sexual feelings of any kind.'

In 1900, Lyman B. Sperry's *Book of Information and Advice for the Married and Marriageable* advised, 'The ordinary man can safely indulge about four times a month. More than that would be excess for a large majority of civilised men and women.'

By 1925, sales of *Married Love* by Marie Stopes had passed the half-million mark, despite the fact that she was a virgin.

The Times, reviewing *You Put WHAT Where?*
Over Two-Thousand Years of Bizarre Sex Advice
by John Naish (Harper Element)

A book by cartoonist Gerald Scarfe called *Drawing Blood*, due to be printed in China, ran into some local difficulty with the thought police, who said there were too many erect willies. Scarfe asked what the problem was and got the reply: 'Too big'.

Scarfe responded: 'Well, that's the way they are over here.'

Independent

Some letters from Wrens and convent pupils told of bygone disciplinary practices involving being spanked on their bare bottoms. This was followed by a missive from a gentleman who wrote, 'They should think themselves lucky. Their discipline came free. I have to pay the elegant young lady, on whom I attend in Chelsea.'

Sunday Telegraph

In March 2006, the TV production *The Chatterley Affair* sparked memories of the sensational 1960 Old Bailey trial when Penguin Books was unsuccessfully prosecuted for publishing DH Lawrence's *Lady Chatterley's Lover*. Mervyn Griffith-Jones, for the prosecution, famously asked the jury if the story of Lady Chatterley's steamy affair with her gamekeeper was something 'you would wish your wife or your servants to read'.

The *Independent* reported that Griffith-Jones once explained how he decided for himself if a book was obscene: 'I put my feet up on the desk and start reading. If I get an erection, we prosecute.'

(After the trial huge queues formed outside bookshops and three million were sold in twelve months.)

Independent

Lady Chatterley was much harder stuff than the naughty songs of the late, great music hall performer Marie Lloyd. She was once upbraided for this line in one of her songs: 'She sits among the cabbages and peas'. She changed it to: 'She sits among the cabbages and leeks'.

The Times magazine *The Knowledge*

When a cast of Michelangelo's David was presented to what is now the Victoria and Albert Museum, it was provided with a detachable fig leaf so that the Queen might not be depraved by the sight of a penis.

Independent on Sunday

Lucy Priory and her secondary-school mates began reading Shakespeare enthusiastically – after a wise young teacher pointed out all the references to sex.

Daily Telegraph

Shakespeare – the bawdy bard. Intensive research for sexual innuendo has found toilet humour and smut buried deep in the national poet's works. Heloise Senechal, working on the footnotes for a new Royal Shakespeare Company edition of the complete works, has found 'more than a hundred terms for vagina alone'.

Shakespeare is 'absolutely packed with sex', says Heloise. She has identified seemingly innocuous words such as carrot, pencil and horn as terms for penis – and pie, fruit dish and 'buggle boe' for vagina.

The *Observer* provides as a sample Mercutio telling Romeo: 'Love is like a great natural that runs lolling [with tongue or penis out [up and down to hide his bauble [fool's baton or penis] in a hole [vagina].'

Shakespeare has been accused of risqué humour before. Dr Johnson deemed *A Midsummer Night's Dream* not the sort of play Elizabeth I should have seen.

Observer

In May 2005, a BBC Radio 4 poll voted the bicycle the greatest technical advance in the past two centuries. But when it first began to have mass appeal in the 1890s Victorian Britain was scandalised. They feared that the bicycle would foster improper liaisons, encourage immodest attire and provide sexual arousal.

Daily Mail

Millionaire Michael Winner wrote of his treasured collection of the work of Donald McGill, king of the saucy seaside postcard. He chose to mention:

- Doctor visiting a sick man asks his wife:
  'I suppose you're giving him all he
  wants?' 'Oh, Doctor, he's been far too ill
  to think about anything of that sort.'
- Buxom housewife says to decorator, 'I
  want you to touch up the place where
  my husband put his hand last night.'
- A couple of old stagers observing newly
  wed couple:
  'They're honeymooners.'
  'Yes, it's sticking out a mile.'
- Postcard of a lady wearing a Union Jack

dress captioned: 'Many a battle has been
fought under this old flag.'

- Neighbour of a woman hanging out her
laundry comments that her nightdress
looks the worse for wear: 'Well, dear, it's
had some ups and downs.'

These naughty jokes may seem innocent now, but
they were occasionally banned in some seaside
resorts and sometimes landed McGill in court.
McGill divided his cards into three categories: mild,
medium and strong. The strong ones sold the best.

Daily Mail

'Craziest parking ticket award'

Chapter 10

Politics: Order, Order!

EU to ban barmaids from showing too much of their boobs?

When a No.10 inquiry cleared Tessa Jowell of breaching the ministerial code, some critics described the inquiry as 'whitewash'. It all reminded James Strachan, of Cambridge, of a defendant in an Irish trial who was found not guilty. The judge said, 'You leave this court with no stain on your character other than that of being acquitted by a Killarney jury.'

Daily Telegraph

In his *News of the World* column, former Tory Party leader William ('He Knows. He's Been There') Hague looked forward to speaking at the party's annual conference in Blackpool, October 2005. 'I was discussing with friends,' he writes, 'the most dramatic possible start to my speech.'

Among the suggestions:

- 'After much reflection I have decided to run again for the leadership... Only kidding.'
- 'I'm in charge for the next fifteen minutes, which I suppose is about average.'

News of the World

A woman once said to Churchill, 'In the year 2000 women will rule the world.'

Winston replied, 'What, still?'

Matthew Dexter, NW5,
Independent

An article on dreams that came true was followed by a letter from Dr Sebastian Kraemer, of London: 'Bertrand Russell's example is of the Duke of Westmorland, who dreamed that he was speaking in the House of Lords and woke up to find that he was.'

Guardian

The father-in-law of Prime Minister Tony Blair is Tony Booth, famous as the 'Scouse git' in *Till Death Do Us Part*. On their first meeting, Booth asked

Blair, 'Do you mind if I smoke a joint?' and Blair said later, 'I remember thinking, this is my father-in-law. This should be the other way round.'

Independent

(Later Tom Kelly, the Prime Minister's official spokesman, wrote to the press saying that Mr Blair refused permission for the joint to be lit in his presence.)

In 1999, the *Daily Mail* made a Dubious Achievement award to Screaming Lord Sutch. He had spent four days by-election canvassing in Richmond, London, before realising that the election was in Richmond, Yorkshire.

Daily Mail

Welsh soprano Charlotte Church says the least impressive celeb she's ever met is George W. Bush, who asked her what state Wales was in.

News of the World

It sounds like something Sir Humphrey Appleby might have said in the TV comedy *Yes Minister*: 'Whitehall has blocked a Freedom of Information request about the workings of the Freedom of Information Act because "the information that might be freed is far too secret for public consumption."'

The Times

All sorts of vital stuff pops up as a result of the Freedom of Information Act. Without it, we might never have got to know that in 1979 Margaret Thatcher's new government was considering importing bottle-nosed dolphins from the United States to seek out the Loch Ness monster.

The Times

The Conservative Party's 2005 Blackpool conference magazine carries an ad for the British Toilet Association which points out that, for many, the lasting impression of any town will be formed by its public toilets. It says: 'GOOD LUCK TO ALL CONSERVATIVES. MAY WE SUGGEST YOU MAKE A POINT OF VISITING ONE OR MORE TOILETS IN THE AREA.'

The Times

Sir Edward Heath, Prime Minister 1970–74, died on 17 July 2005, aged 89. He was bitter when Margaret Thatcher replaced him as Tory party leader and went into what has been called 'the longest sulk in history'. Filmmaker Michael Cockerell asked Heath if it was true that when Thatcher fell from power in 1990 he rang his office and said, 'Rejoice, rejoice.' Heath replied, 'No, that's completely untrue. I rang my office and said, "Rejoice, rejoice, rejoice."'

Cockerell comments, 'It was a classic deadpan Heath remark.'

Guardian

Heath is fondly remembered for an incident during the 1974 election campaign. The campaign bus braked sharply and an aide was thrown out of her seat. She pluckily insisted that the bus should carry on but Heath would have none of it. 'No, no,' he said, 'we must get some brandy.'

A glass of brandy was brought from a nearby pub and Ted drank the lot.

Sunday Times

A Churchillian chestnut of apocrypha has him asking a grand lady if she would sleep with him for £1 million. The lady says she would have to give the matter serious thought.

Churchill: Would you sleep with me for £5?

Grand Lady: How dare you? What do you think I am?

Churchill: We have established what you are. It only remains for us to agree a price.

Keith Waterhouse, *Daily Mail*

From the fun-loving free marketers at the Adam Smith Institute: How many government ministers does it take to change a light bulb?
Answer: That's not the real issue here. The important point is that light bulbs are being changed far more efficiently than they were under the previous Tory government.

Sunday Times

"Dog" is one of the terms of abuse specifically listed as unparliamentary and MPs may not use it of one another. "Impertinent puppy" is another.'

Daily Express

Denis McShane, Labour MP for Rotherham, tells the *New Statesman* magazine that he is the only Privy Councillor who has been picked up by police for smuggling. In 1982, he was apprehended by Polish Police after smuggling money to the underground union Solidarity. When he was being held in prison, the British Embassy sent along the 'standard Foreign Office survival kit – a Harrods' bag containing three apples, a jar of Marmite, a packet of Ryvita and two copies of *Country Life* magazine'.

Ephraim Hardcastle's column, *Daily Mail*

Simon Hoggart met a US serviceman who told of his visit to the House of Lords. Needing the bathroom, he went through a door marked 'Peers'. 'When I got in there,' said the soldier, 'there was this old guy who said, "Do you realise that this is for peers only?" and I said, "But that's all I want to do."'

Guardian

Within days of winning the 2005 general election the new Labour government announced that the Department for Trade and Industry would be renamed the Department for Productivity, Energy and Industry – and almost immediately changed its mind. The *Financial Times* called it all a Whitehall farce that would not be out of place in *Yes Minister*.

The new Secretary of State for the department, Alan Johnson, complained that the new title attracted unwelcome acronyms – 'penis' for him and 'dippy' for the department. One government official blamed the name switch on 'an administrative cock-up'.

Financial Times

On the day Margaret Thatcher became Leader of the Opposition her husband Denis turned up, on time as usual, at his desk at Burmah Oil. He remained his own man, appreciated his wife's achievement, but was not dazzled by it. 'Margaret has a temporary job,' he once remarked.

Libby Purves in *The Times*

The Times reports that a rebellious, politically incorrect, obese, heavy-drinking schools failure, who smoked and did dodgy deals with dictators, has been nominated as Britain's greatest all-time hero. The report was referring, of course, to Sir Winston Churchill.

Alan Hamilton in *The Times*

Top Tories rarely enjoy raffish Blackpool as the venue for their annual party conference. Their former social security secretary Peter Lilley once asked where the bathroom was at his B&B and the landlady said, 'Didn't you have a bath before you came, love?'

Daily Mail

Granita, the trendy Islington restaurant famous as the location where Gordon Brown is reported to have agreed to step aside in the 1994 Labour Party leadership contest has become a Tex-Mex establishment called Desperados.

Jack Winkler, London, *Guardian*

Lord (David) Sainsbury, one of the richest men in the country and a member of Labour's government team, was canvassing in the Hammersmith & Fulham constituency during the 2005 general election. One voter answered his knock on the door and asked, 'Are you from the supermarket?'

'In a way, I am,' replied his lordship.

'Well, where the hell are my groceries? Either deliver them when you say you are going to, or give me my money back.'

The seat turned out to be one of those that the Tories won back from Labour.

Sunday Telegraph

When Michael Howard went to do a spot of by-election campaigning in the affluent seat of Cheadle in Cheshire in July 2005, he addressed the students of Kingsway School – from a chair placed in the fiction section of the library.

Guardian

Duff Cooper was one of the most influential men of his age, a friend of royalty, confidant of Winston Churchill, Secretary of State for War in Stanley Baldwin's cabinet, British ambassador in Paris – and an insatiable womaniser. Throughout his marriage to Lady Diana Manners, he enjoyed the favours of high-class mistresses and wrote of one of them, 'She is a girl after my own heart with a formidable appetite for pleasure and no nonsense about love. She has four children, feels she has done her duty and is now determined to have a good time. I shall do my best to help her.'

From the Duff Cooper Diaries 1915–57, edited by his son John Julius Norwich and published by Weidenfeld & Nicholson.

Daily Mail

During the 2005 election campaign, Tony Blair tested the fare in 'Tony's' fish and chip shop in Rochdale, Lancashire, and asked, 'Which one of you is Tony?'

'Er, Tony's retired,' was the reply.

Ephraim Hardcastle, *Daily Mail*

Former Labour Prime Minister Clement Attlee was the butt of many of Churchill's best insults such as: 'An empty taxi arrived at 10 Downing Street and, when the door was opened, Attlee got out.'

However, Clem could give as good as he got. When asked how Churchill won the war, Attlee replied, 'He talked about it.'

Diarist Giles Foden, *Guardian*

As the Labour Party's 2005 conference in Brighton was talking about getting tough on crime, police in Farnborough, Hampshire, chipped in with their own pennyworth of advice on how to beat burglars: 'Take Your Valuables to Bed With You'.

Daily Telegraph

At the 2005 Labour Party conference in Brighton, Cherie Blair outed the first boy with whom she shared a childhood kiss. It was with Stephen Smerdon, who became a pub landlord and was happy to recall the tender moment: 'It was my first kiss. It was her first kiss. We didn't have a clue what we were doing.' They were both 11.

The story, inevitably, sparked a search for Tony Blair's first kiss. The *Sunday Telegraph* tracked down the girl believed to be the one – the former Miss Amanda Mackenzie-Stuart, the first girl pupil at Fettes College. The *Sunday Telegraph* reported that the Prime Minister and Amanda were not keen to reveal the location of their first kiss – 'possibly behind the bike shed at Fettes'.

Amanda said, 'How would I know if I was the first girl to kiss him?'

Sunday Telegraph

WF Deedes records in his Notebook an item from Gerry Hanson's book England, My England: 'The Lords Prayer contains sixty-nine words. The Ten Commandments 297. The American Declaration of Independence 310 words. The EU directive on exporting duck eggs – 28,911 words.'

Daily Telegraph

The Press Office of the European Commission in London – with an almost audible sigh – says of the above duck-egg story, 'The origins of this story are unclear, but the matter of a regulation on the export of duck eggs has been widely used by Eurosceptic organisations and several times in the House of Lords by Lord Harris of High Cross, as long ago as June 1997. However, we have never been able to track down any such specific legislation.'

For a long list of Euro-myths debunked by the Commission, go to: www.cec.org.uk/press/index.htm. It tackles such stories as:

- EU to ban barmaids revealing too much of their boobs.
- Butchers banned from selling bones for dogs.

- Trapeze artists must wear hard hats.
- Bagpipes face the axe under noise pollution rules.
- Condom dimensions to be harmonised.
- Kilts are women's wear.
- Bananas and rhubarb must be straight.

In December 2005, Tony Blair told the *Daily Mirror* that he would not go to the House of Lords after stepping down from the Prime Minister's job. The *Daily Mail* then reminded us that Mr Blair was following the example of Winston Churchill, Edward Heath and John Major 'who all balked at joining the riff-raff they'd sent to the Lords'.

Daily Mail

John Sergeant was the BBC's chief political correspondent from 1992 to 2000. In 2005, he had a cameo role in the children's TV comedy *My Dad's the Prime Minister*. It involved him standing outside a mock-up of Downing Street, and the BBC paid him 'far more for pretending to be myself than they ever did for actually being myself'.

Guardian

MP George Galloway took a lot of stick for taking part in *Celebrity Big Brother*. Columnist Nigel Farndale wrote, 'Imagine how he must have felt when he swaggered into "the house" and discovered that, of his eleven fellow celebrities, only one knew who he was. The closest any of them came was when a 22-year-old said, "You work in that place with the green seats, don'tcha?'"

Sunday Telegraph

Tory Leader David Cameron's son was born in February 2006. Within days, William Hill were offering odds on the boy:

- Going to Eton – 2/1, later cut to evens.
- Becoming a future Tory Party leader – 66/1.
- Becoming a future Labour Party leader – 200/1.
- Having his name tattooed on either of his parents – 250/1.

Sun

Winston Churchill shares a problem with Kylie Minogue. Kylie's waxwork in Madame Tussauds suffers from wear because fans cannot resist stroking certain parts. Winston has an imposing statue adorning the Members' Lobby of the House of Commons. For thirty-five years, his admirers have not been able to resist stroking his protruding left foot. (Tory MPs in particular would give it a rub 'for good luck' on their way into important debates.) So much so that the bronze surface of the foot has been gradually worn away.

In March 2006 guides were told to discourage the practice, but a realistic Westminster official admitted that it was going to be very difficult to stop people paying their respects to the old warrior.

Daily Telegraph

It was the start of the Click for the Climate campaign and No. 10 was keen to demonstrate Labour's green credentials by putting a low-energy bulb in the lamp outside the famous door. Much energy was spent on the great occasion. Attending the ceremony were three PR officers, two policemen, one engineer to hold the ladder and another one to put the bulb in.

Across the road, the House of Commons was busy tightening up on security and MPs were invited to a talk entitled: 'Become An Instant Expert! Improvised Explosive Devices. Please Note: This is not a practical demonstration session.'

Sun

'All babies are supposed to look like me – at both ends.'
Winston Churchill

'Thank goodness he hasn't got ears like his father.'
The Queen, on first seeing Prince William
From *Fathers'* Wit by Rosemarie Jarski (Prion)

At a dinner party in Washington DC, Margaret Thatcher was asked what she thought of developments in Europe. She then launched into a caustic indictment of European integration. With eyes blazing, she began to bang on a bit until a voice rang out: 'Enough, woman, sit down!'

It was Denis Thatcher. His wife meekly obeyed.

From the memoirs of former
UK ambassador Sir Christopher Meyer,
serialised in the *Daily Mail*

Huge controversy followed some of the revelations in Sir Christopher's memoirs. But John Nevis, of Broseley, Shropshire, spotted something to really upset English gentlemen. 'Surely,' he wrote, 'nobody should be so naive as to expect discretion from a man whose tie matches his socks.'

Guardian

'In June 2005 there were 250 100-year-old motorists still driving'

Chapter 11

Wedded Bliss

Secret of successful marriage:
always say 'Yes dear'...

'Witch guide to divorce, used once.'
Spotted in the Seaford Friday Ad
by R. E. Fisher of Brighton

A *Daily Mail* reader tells of the day (in Wales during the
sixties) when his wife popped some cakes into the oven
and decided to run a bath while they were baking. She
undressed in the bathroom and then nipped downstairs
to see how the cakes were doing. While naked in the
kitchen, she heard the latch on the door and a shout of
'Hello. Good Morning.'

She thought it would be the breadman who would

normally leave her order on the kitchen table. She popped out of sight into the cupboard under the stairs and then suddenly the cupboard door opened.

'I'm not sure,' writes her husband, 'who got the biggest surprise – the meter man or my wife, particularly as all she could think of to say was, "Oh! I was expecting the breadman."'

Daily Mail

A Pontypridd husband assaulted his wife because she bought the wrong kind of baked beans.

Independent on Sunday

Following an article on helpless husbands, Mrs Yaffa Glass, of Leeds, writes, 'None of the husbands described is quite as helpless as our friend who, when shopping for shoes, put on a new pair and asked his wife: "Are they comfortable?"'

The Times

Bigamy is still thriving, with seventy-one offences in 2003 (down from an inexplicable high of 129 in 1998). Helen Rumbelow in *The Times* writes that many of the cases are full of human comedy and points out that in the case of the man who deceived two wives, he decorated their houses in identical wallpaper and furnishings to save on costs.

When the men of Alston, Cumberland (population 1,000) lamented the shortage of women in the village, a local lad said that he was looking for one 'who likes conversation and knows about tractors'.

Sunday Telegraph

A Bristol businesswoman has set up a service to help women of 'high net worth' through the pain of separation and divorce. The only qualification required is a £1 million-plus divorce settlement.

The Times

In June 2005, Percy and Florence Arrowsmith of Hereford celebrated their 80th wedding anniversary and achieved the world record for the longest marriage. When they married, Stanley Baldwin was Prime Minister, beer was 5d a pint, the Charleston was all the rage, Charlie Chaplin made *The Gold Rush*, George V was on the throne, Winston Churchill was Chancellor and knocked sixpence off income tax. Percy, 105, was a solicitor's clerk and sang in the local church choir. Florence, 100, was a Sunday schoolteacher.

She says: 'We don't argue much these days – except when I want to watch the soaps... But before we go to sleep we always make up with a kiss and a cuddle.'

He says the secret of a successful partnership is to always say 'Yes dear'.

Daily Telegraph/Sun/Guardian

For 20 years, from her home in Bakewell, Derbyshire, Patricia Warren has run a successful dating agency called the Farmers and Country Bureau. It helps rural people find love, but on the odd occasion throws up a difficulty. She tells this story in a book she has written called *Tales from a Country Matchmaker*.

George, a Yorkshireman, rang to say, 'That lass you fixed me up wi', she's no bloody good. Too tight wi' her money.'

Patricia said if George didn't want to see the lady again he should tell her so. George then said he didn't want to do that straight away because 'she's knitting me a jumper. So I canna finish wi' her till it's all joined up, else it'll be a waste o' good wool. Don't worry, I'll tell her when t' jumper's finished.'

Patricia's book is published by Hodder & Stoughton *Daily Telegraph*

Hamish Hardie, of Kilmacolm, Renfrewshire, tells of the time, in 1954, when he rang his Edinburgh-based fiancée from Calgary, Alberta. Telephone calls were by landline across Canada and then by cable under the Atlantic. They were barely audible and at one stage his fiancée asked, 'What did you say?' Immediately, the Montreal operator came in with: 'He says he loves you', which was then repeated by operators in London and Edinburgh.

'It seemed to work,' Hamish writes. 'We celebrated our golden wedding last month [June 2005]'.

The Times

The Times carried a series of letters about wives who compiled lists of jobs for their husbands to do. One husband wrote that if his wife died before him he would have engraved on her tombstone: 'She finally reached the end of her list'.

Another husband wrote that his wife was planning to inscribe his tombstone: 'He's in there somewhere' in revenge for his usual response to her asking where something is.

A third also faced tombstone revenge. His wife, infuriated for years by his nodding off in front of the TV, decided on this epitaph: 'Beloved Husband. Fallen Asleep Again.'

A wife with a tidy husband said he would have his favourite saying on his tombstone: 'A place for everything and everything in its place'.

A Londoner writes to say that her husband insists on inserting commas into her writings. She has informed him that his epitaph is to be: 'He loved his commas, but now he has come to a full stop'.

A Harbury, Warwickshire, husband says his wife has a tendency towards stress and anxiety and he has told her that her tombstone will read: 'Relaxed at last'.

The Times

86-year-old Ruth Bloxham celebrated her 65th wedding anniversary with her husband Joseph (also 86) and said, 'We got married on Battle of Britain Day in 1940 and it's been like that ever since.'

Spotted by Roy Gillard in the
Birmingham Evening Mail

Nicola Bell and Charlie Adie got married in Hazelwood Castle, North Yorkshire, and their wedding cake was a three-tiered pork pie (the bride's dad is a butcher). The wedding breakfast menu included fish and chips, sausage and mash and haggis.

The Times

So many couples getting married these days have already lived with each other for so long that they already have all the items that used to go on wedding-present lists. The John Lewis department store reported in 2006 that popular items on wedding lists now include swimming goggles, giant dominoes, skateboards, body-fat monitors – and gumshields and punchbags.

Daily Telegraph

Women have taken over thousands of allotment plots and now often outnumber men on waiting lists. Not everybody is happy about this, particularly those men who still regard allotments as a male preserve and 'somewhere to get away from the wife'. One such male grumbled, 'Allotments used to be just vegetable patches but now they have flowers, ponds and lawns.' Worse than this – women are accused of introducing garden furniture and putting up curtains in their sheds.

Daily Telegraph

The enduring love between the Queen and Prince Philip lives on. During a three-day break at a tourist attraction in Canada in 2005, staff revealed that, although they slept in separate rooms, they had photographs of each other placed on their bedside tables.

Daily Mail

Jack and Helen Hope were married for seventy years and they always said that each would not be able to go on living without the other. Mr Hope, 98, died in hospital in March 2006. Minutes later, Mrs Hope, 94, passed away in a different ward of Ipswich Hospital.

Daily Mail

Women are increasingly taking over DIY tasks around the house – claiming they are better at it than men. A survey by Halifax's home insurance arm showed that a record 5.3 million UK women believe they are the best person in the house at DIY. However, the Halifax study shows that men are begrudging about the ability of their partners. Only one in ten agreed that their other half does a better job.

Daily Mail

Chapter 12

What's Up, Doc?

**Soap opera fans go sick at the same
time as their TV heroes...**

Mrs Joyce Urch, of Coventry, lost nearly all her sight in 1979. Miraculously, her sight was restored after she suffered a heart attack in 2005 and she said to her husband, 'You've got older.'

*Coventry Evening Telegraph/
Independent on Sunday*

83-year-old Bill Boyd of Winchester, Hampshire, went to hospital following a minor car crash to have his sore neck checked out. He then learned that he had been living with a broken neck since he parachuted from a burning Lancaster bomber during World War II – sixty-two years ago.

Sun/Daily Mail

When comedian Eric Morecambe had a heart attack in Leeds, a passer-by drove him to hospital. As Eric was being wheeled into intensive care, the man bent over him and asked, 'Can I have your autograph before you go?'

Independent on Sunday

Doctors are having problems giving injections because British bottoms are getting fatter. Soaring obesity means needles aren't always long enough and medics say that longer needles 'are unlikely to be terribly popular'.

Daily Mail

The Accident and Emergency department of York Hospital has reduced the number of attacks on staff by posting cardboard cutouts of policemen that can be easily seen throughout the reception area. 'They have a calming effect,' says chief executive Jim Easton.

Daily Telegraph

A doctor from Nottingham wrote to the *Guardian* in September 2005 saying that his mother believed vegetables made her ill, so she never ate any. 'She died recently aged 95.'

After weeks of freedom an escaped convict was admitted to Guys Hospital in London for a heart operation. He woke up after the op to find cops at his bedside because surgeons had recognised him from TV's *Crimewatch* programme.

Sun

A woman took a telephone call from a dentist's receptionist who wanted to remind the woman's husband about the time of his dental appointment. The husband was out so the wife asked the receptionist to give the time to her. Not possible, said the receptionist – because of the Data Protection Act. However, guessing to establish the correct day was allowed.

Daily Telegraph

A medical dictionary is being compiled for doctors whose training has not prepared them for the dialect of the North East. For newcomers to the region it is important to know that:

- 'Wor lass's moonging she's fallen wrang' means: our daughter thinks she's pregnant.
- 'The gadgie's cakky's in the gazunder' means: granddad's sample is in this pot.
- 'Ah'm flaid its lops agin' means: the kids have got nits, not for the first time.

- 'It's me neb. It's all bubbly' means: my nose is snotty.
- 'A mardy gob oil' indicates mouth ulcers.
- 'Trollibags' are intestines.

The Times/Guardian

TV soap-opera fans often get the real lives of the actors mixed up with the roles they play. But some go a bit further than that according to a survey by Norwich Union Healthcare: 95% of GPs claimed to have had patients reporting symptoms of the illnesses affecting their fictional screen heroes – such as *EastEnder* Dot Cotton's struggle with kidney cancer.

Guardian/Daily Mail

A phenomenon which sounds like science fiction is intriguing medical experts. Is it possible that, during an organ transplant, the recipient can inherit character traits from the donor? Cases cited by researchers include:

- A woman who was terrified of heights was given the lung of a mountain climber and became a climber herself.
- A man who was given the heart of a 14-year-old boy developed a craving for Snickers.
- A man of 25 who received a woman's heart became a keen shopper.

152

- A man with no artistic ability got the heart of an artist – and discovered he had the skill to produce colourful and elaborate paintings.

Daily Mail

The *British Journal of Psychiatry* published research suggesting that if you live in the country you have less chance of being barmy than if you live in a town or city. The researchers must be bonkers, says countrywoman Kishanda Fulford. What about:

The Duke of Portland, who constructed an entire underground ballroom, riding stable and a drive more than a mile long at his Welbeck house to ensure he never had to see anyone.

Lord Leconfield, who built an extremely expensive greenhouse at Petworth so that he could grow bananas. When his butler delivered the first homegrown banana on a silver salver his lordship said, 'Tastes like any other damn banana'.

Sherlock Homes, who said that 'the lowest and vilest alleys of London do not present a more dreadful record of sin than does the smiling and beautiful countryside'.

Substitute the word 'pottiness' for 'sin' and Sherlock's claim would be a pretty accurate quote for today, says Kishanda.

Daily Mail

'A lucky escape'

Chapter 13

Driven to Distraction

Postman Pat branded as a dangerous driver...

The number of women drivers convicted of speeding has risen by almost a quarter in five years – possibly because speed cameras are less susceptible to their charms than are male police officers.

The Times

Tired of tailgaters, R. S. Darke, of Princess Risborough, Buckinghamshire, and a friend have a rear-window car sticker which shows a tortoise and the message: 'Nine Points. That's Why'.

The Times

Donna Maddock, 22, from Mold in North Wales, was fined £200 for applying make-up while driving at 32mph. 'It is what I would call one of my blonde moments,' she said.

Western Mail

Norwich Union has a collection of the most novel claims made by drivers. Among them: 'A herd of cows licked my car and damaged the paintwork'.

Independent on Sunday

Stubborn male drivers take twice as long as women to admit that they are lost. According to a survey by RAC Direct Insurance, men waste nearly six million hours a year through their reluctance to stop and ask for help. They will spend an average of twenty minutes before giving up and seeking directions. Women stop and ask in about ten minutes.

Scotsman/Metro

A Teignmouth, Devon, man was given a two-year ASBO after tricking women into taking off their tights. He pretended he wanted them to repair his fan belt.

The Times

Rachel Farthing was lost on the M6. She saw a parked police car and pulled over to ask for directions. She got the directions, but not before being booked for unauthorised use of the hard shoulder and fined £30.

Independent on Sunday

David Gethyn-Jones was driving out of Bristol Airport when the car behind gently shunted into him. The driver explained that he had been distracted by a large sign reading: 'Bristol International wishes you a safe onward journey'.

Daily Mail

Sign on garage door next to Harpsden Church near Henley on Thames:

THOU SHALT NOT PARK IN THY NEIGHBOUR'S SPACE.

Henley Standard

In the twelve months to April 2005, motorists were hit with more than £3 million in parking tickets in Brixton's 400-metre Atlantic Road.

Evening Standard

Urban drivers of 4x4s ('Chelsea Tractors') can pretend they have been in rough country by spraying their vehicles with genuine Shropshire mud available in a squirt-bottle costing £7.95.

Guardian/The Times

Owners of 4x4s have long had to live with the sneers of other road users... That's because the nearest they'll get to dirt is a puddle in the Tesco car park.

Daily Mail

At the age of 50, Vera Crabtree, of Oxford, passed her driving test, after forty attempts over thirty-three years – having spent some £27,000 on lessons with seven different instructors.

Independent on Sunday

Someone in the UK fills a diesel vehicle with petrol 400 times a day.

The Times

Jason Evans, 34, was fined £150 and given three penalty points after driving through a puddle and splashing a road worker in Yeovil Somerset.

Ian Richards, 29, of Warrington, Cheshire, was fined £30 for hooting to tell another driver it was safe to go.

Marcus Aitken, 30, of Manchester, was fined £30 for playing 'Riverdance' too loud in his car.

Sarah McCaffery, 23, of Tyneside, was fined £60 after a police helicopter videoed her holding an apple at the wheel.

Celia Pearce, 48, was given a £30 fixed penalty fine in Alton, Hampshire, for putting a 'For Sale' sign on her windscreen. Her ticket said, 'Sale of Goods is not allowed in council car parks'. (The local council said the ticket would be cancelled and added, 'Our attendant followed the letter of the parking order, but not the spirit.')

Sun

Postman Pat has ended up on a list of 'dangerous drivers' in an analysis of cartoon characters who would not be welcomed by insurers. Top of the Churchill insurance company's list of Toon Terrors is:

- Dick Dastardly, of Wacky Races, who 'would struggle to find anybody to insure him in real life'.
- Second most uninsurable cartoon character is Homer Simpson – guilty of road rage, sleeping behind the wheel, obesity, poor eyesight and a tendency to eat donuts while driving.
- Noddy is fifth – guilty of driving into Big Ears's bike and illegally using his car as a taxi.
- Postman Pat, who carries too many expensive items, is eighth.

The Times

Don Astwood, 62, had his car stolen from outside his home near Rochdale. It was recovered and taken to a local compound, but when Mr Astwood went to reclaim the car, West Yorkshire police demanded £200. He is not alone. Thousands of motorists who have their cars stolen are being forced to pay to get them back.

Tory spokesman Nick Herbert says: 'This is unfair to victims of crime. The last thing you expect if you have your car stolen is to have to pay for the privilege.'

Daily Mail

You can be too polite. Robert Vincent and his wife were dawdling near a zebra crossing in Salisbury. A lady driver sounded her horn and indicated that they should cross. Mr Vincent waved her on, but the driver insisted. His wife, anxious not to cause offence, dragged her husband across. The driver blew her horn angrily because they had failed to thank her. The Vincents waited until the car turned a corner before they dared cross back.

'Politeness,' writes Mr Vincent, 'can be a pain.'

The Times

Speed cameras in West Yorkshire now have other cameras spying on them. The 'spy' cameras are there to trap vandals who use spray paint to blind the speed cameras and sometimes set them on fire. One was badly damaged when a motorist deliberately rammed it.

Sunday Times

In-car satellite navigation systems were criticised by people who thought they distracted drivers' attention. Fans wrote in saying that they found them safe and wonderful. Chris Lambert of Tadworth, Surrey, wrote, 'The question pales into insignificance if the number of marriages that satnav devices have saved is taken into account.'

Daily Telegraph

Chapter 14

Not Dead, Just Resting

Erith isn't twinned with anywhere, but it has a suicide pact with Dagenham...

Terry Wogan tells of the woman who kept her mother's ashes on the mantelpiece. Her husband took to knocking the remains of his pipe into the urn. A priest, who was a regular visitor, lifted the lid of the urn and said, 'Mother's putting on weight.'

Sunday Telegraph

Radio 4's *Today* programme told of a woman who had her husband's ashes put into a timer which she kept by the cooker. 'When the ashes run out,' she said, 'I know the meat is cooked. I've got him working at last!'

The memorial service for comedian Ronnie Barker was held in Westminster Cathedral in March 2006. His partner Ronnie Corbett delivered the eulogy and remembered a time when he was working with Barker and Harry Secombe (both somewhat portly gentlemen who were trying to lose weight). 'One night at dinner,' said the diminutive Corbett, 'we came to the conclusion that, between them, they had lost the equivalent of me.'

The Times

There was some surprise when Lady Thatcher attended the funeral of her old enemy Sir Edward Heath. David Collins, of Kidderminster, Worcestershire, said it reminded him of four reasons for attending a funeral:
- As an expression of grief.
- An indication of sympathy with the family.
- As a matter of duty.
- To make sure the bastard's really dead.

Independent/Sunday Times

Tony Banks (Lord Stratford) died on 8 January 2006. He was an East End Labour MP for twenty-two years and *The Times* obituary called him 'almost a caricature of the chirpy, cheeky Cockney portrayed in British feelgood films of a bygone age'.

The obituary quotes a typical Banksian riposte (on former Prime Minister John Major): 'He is so unpopular that if he became a funeral director people would stop dying.'

The Times

A survey by Age Concern found many people wanted their mobile phones to be buried with them.

Guardian

Death didn't stop Ernie Cross, 73, from hanging around his local pub. Ernie was a regular at the Hatters Arms in Marple, Greater Manchester. The landlord used his ashes as fertiliser in the pub's hanging baskets – and the Hatters won a Best Pub in Bloom competition. Other regulars admire the prize-winning flower baskets and say, 'Ernie's looking well.'

Daily Mail

The English have a strange love for the flamboyant funerals laid on for their top criminals. In Manchester in April 2005, hundreds turned out to pay their last respects to notorious crime enforcer Desmond 'Dessie' Noonan. Traffic came to a standstill as a traditional kilted pipe band led the way, followed by four black-plumed horses drawing the carriage carrying Noonan's body. A cortege of twelve black Daimler cars was weighed down with sentimental floral tributes, including one spelling out the words 'The Boss'.

The Times reported that the Noonans come from

a large and well-known Irish family and 'represent underworld royalty'. The Noonan brothers were in the thick of gang wars in the 80s, which caused Manchester to be dubbed Gunchester. Noonan, 46, boasted that he had 'a bigger army than the police'.

The Times/Daily Telegraph

Britain's heaviest man, Chris McGarva, 35, who weighed 65st, was buried in a coffin 6ft 6in long, 4ft wide and weighing half a ton. It had to be lowered into his grave at Grantham, Lincolnshire, by crane.

Sun

After her father died, Sheila Lane, of Hook in Hampshire, was told by Barclay's bank that it could not close her dad's account without his signature. She took the casket bearing his ashes to the local branch, slammed it on to the counter and said, 'If you think you can get a signature out of him then you are a better person than me.'

The bank apologised for 'a clerical error' and sent Mrs Lane a bouquet.

Daily Telegraph

A *Times* reader received a phone call from a man she suspected was going to try to sell her some double glazing or a fitted kitchen. She slammed the phone down. A few minutes later, the man was on the phone again saying that he was not a salesman but was 'actually, your vicar, and I was wondering if we could borrow your donkey for our Nativity services'.

The Times

Jenny Saxby, of Selly Park, Birmingham, tells *The Times* of a kind, thoughtful maiden aunt who left an envelope to be opened on her death. When the time came, the letter led them to another envelope – tucked between the dust bag and the outer casing of her vacuum cleaner. It contained sufficient cash to pay funeral expenses.

The Times

'Coffins are so last century' – headline on a story about how a group of experts on death and dying met in Bath and disclosed some unusual funeral arrangements which people are requesting:

- Ashes placed in a capsule and launched into orbit.
- 'Cremain' paintings in which cremated remains are mixed with oil paints and daubed on giant canvases.
- Remains scattered over a coral reef.

- Cyberspace cemeteries – websites where family and friends leave virtual messages for the dead.
- Having a solar-powered video embedded in your tombstone.
- Arranging for your pallbearers to be dressed as Elvis.

Guardian

Scattering the ashes of loved ones on mountaintops is becoming so popular that, instead of being bleak and bare, they are becoming lush and green. The ashes contain nourishing phosphates and plants are thriving as never before in the enriched soil.

The Times

Linda Smith, the comedian who died in February 2006 aged 48. She was a sharp-tongued veteran of BBC Radio's *News Quiz* and I'*m Sorry I Haven't a Clue* – born to a working-class home in Erith, Kent. She said of Erith, 'It isn't twinned with anywhere, but it does have a suicide pact with Dagenham.'

Independent

Linda [Smith] did many a benefit show on behalf of the striking miners back in the mid-80s. She loved the story about a police Land Rover that smashed down a snowman built by the picketing miners. 'Next day the miners built another snowman and the same thing happened. What the police didn't know was that the second snowman was built round a cast iron bollard.'

Guardian

'A pretty odd-looking character'

Chapter 15

Raise Your Glasses

Today's binge drinkers are beginners compared with Hogarth's 18th-century London...

At a grand reception in Peru during the 1960s, George Brown, then Foreign Secretary, approached a guest wearing a purple frock and asked for a dance. He was turned down with this response: 'First, you are drunk. Second, this is not a waltz, it is the Peruvian national anthem. And, third, I am not a woman, I am the Cardinal Archbishop of Lima.'

The Times

In January 2006, Charles Kennedy admitted he had a drink problem and resigned as the leader of the Liberal

Democrats. Veteran political commentator Alan Watkins wrote, 'By the standards of consumption of the great men of Old Fleet Street among whom I was lucky enough to grow up... Mr Kennedy's intake always struck me as being on the moderate side.'

Independent on Sunday

- William Pitt the Younger marinated himself daily with three bottles of port.
- Winston Churchill slurped through the war on a tidal wave of champagne and brandy. He said, 'I have taken more out of alcohol than it has taken out of me.'
- Asquith was known as Squiffy.
- The phrase 'tired and emotional' was coined for George Brown.
- There are seventeen places to buy alcohol in the Palace of Westminster, which is immune from legal restrictions on closing times.

The Times

In an article about binge drinkers, an ex-licensee gave his views on twenty-four-hour drinking laws and said, 'Instead of drinkers spilling out on to the streets all at the same time, crowds will be staggered.'

Liverpool Daily Post

Police in the genteel Sussex resort of Worthing hit upon a novel solution to a plague of late-night binge drinkers disturbing the weekend peace. They moved in with a police van blasting out Classic FM. The operatic arias and string quartets proved too much for the noisy yobs and they moved on. This police strategy was called Operation Brahms and Liszt (Cockney slang for being pissed).

Mail on Sunday

Kim Rule, joint licensee of the Grebe pub in Stalham, Norfolk, gave police a description of the man who burgled her pub. The police produced an e-fit picture of the suspect which made it appear that the burglary had been 'committed by a Martian with a partially severed ear and a stick-on moustache from a Christmas cracker'.

Mrs Rule said that her burglar 'was a pretty odd-looking character – but not as odd as that. I don't think I have ever seen anyone who looks like that in Stalham, or anywhere else, in my life.'

The Times

Inspired by reminders that drinking wine is recommended in the Bible and that Judges ix, 13 says that 'wine cheereth God and man', Graham Darlow, of Finchampstead, Berkshire, writes, 'I hope that when my time comes I am served a decent claret, rather than that usually offered by God's representatives on Earth.'

The Times

British people know so little about wine that many of them think that 'oaked' means that acorns are used as flavouring. Some think that only fat grapes are used in 'full-bodied' wines. Others believe that 'appellation' means 'a combination of apples and grapes'. From a survey for McWilliams, the Australian winemakers.

The Times

On 31 July 2005, Stuart Ashby, from Shoreham-by-Sea, West Sussex, completed a twenty-one-year pub crawl, having visited all 5,054 pubs listed in the 1984 edition of CAMRA's *Good Beer Guide*.

Daily Telegraph/Banterrif internet newsletter

A *Times* reader asked: 'How many inns claim to be the oldest in England?' One reply, from Tim Mickleburgh, of Grimsby, included:

- The Fighting Cocks in St Albans is an 11th-century structure on an 8th-century site.
- The Bingley Arms at Bardsey, near Leeds, existed as the Priest's Inn in 905.
- Ye Olde Ferry Boat Inn, Holywell, Cambridgeshire, allegedly dates from 560.
- The Royalist in Stow-on-the-Wold, Gloucestershire, was known to exist in 947.

The Times

Gordon White, 80, and Tony Smith, 83, claim to be Britain's longest-serving drinking pals – after fifty-three years boozing together. They became neighbours in 1953 and have been out together virtually every day since, downing around 112,000 pints each. They drink half a dozen beers daily in the Dorset Knob, Poole, Dorset, and say, 'We spend hours putting the world to rights.'

Sun

A ban on smoking in public places began to operate in Scotland in March 2006. Pubs there provided tags for customers to put over their beverages reading: 'Please don't take my drink. I've just popped out for a smoke.'

The Times

The perils of binge drinking are seldom out of the papers these days. But today's bingers seem like beginners when you consider Hogarth's 18th-century London, 'a society entirely devoted to drink'. Sir Walter Besant, a novelist writing 100 years later, reports:

- The drinking of the last century went far beyond anything recorded. All classes drank.
- The clergy, merchants, lawyers, judges, the most responsible people, drank more than freely.
- The lowest classes spent all their money

173

on drink, especially gin, upon which
they could get drunk for tuppence.
• They all began to drink hard about 1730
and they kept it up for a hundred years –
with great spirit and admirable results.

Richard Bundy, of London W2,
Daily Telegraph

When shopping malls started banning youths wearing 'hoodies', 82-year-old Betty Wilbraham never thought the rule would extend to her. But the crackdown originally aimed at hoodie-wearing lager louts marred the retired teacher's visit to the Hereward pub in Ely, Cambridgeshire. When Betty popped in for a lunchtime half of Guinness and a plate of fish and chips, she did not notice the new No Hats sign. She went up to the bar wearing a black hat with a maroon ribbon and was told to take it off 'for security reasons'.

She did what she was told because 'I did not want to make a fuss and I don't like to disobey orders. But I am a hat person... My mother wouldn't have set a foot outside the house to go for a loaf of bread without her hat. She would have been horrified if ladies went to lunch without their hats.'

David Sapsted in the *Daily Telegraph*

Chapter 16

School's Out

5-year-old girl gets the clap at school...

Ann Foster of Hull writes that when her daughter Glenda was a child she used to play cards with her granny. When the girl started school, her class practised counting up to ten and one day the teacher asked if anybody knew what came after ten. 'Jack, Queen, King,' replied Glenda.

Daily Mail

Marsha Head, of Stoke, Devonshire, invited a prospective piano pupil to try out a concert grand. 'Where do I switch it on?' the pupil asked.

The Times

Here's what teachers thought of pupils who turned out to be somewhat better than their early school reports indicated:

- Winston Churchill – Constantly late for school. Loses his books and papers. So regular in his irregularity I don't know what to do.
- Albert Einstein – Dullard.
- Robert Graves – Remember your best friend is the waste paper basket.
- Eric Morecambe – Will never get anywhere in life.
- Charlotte Brontë – Writes indifferently. Knows nothing of grammar.
- Gary Lineker – Devote less time to sport. You can't make a living out of football.

From the book *Could Do Better*, published to raise funds for the Dyslexia Institute.

Sun

Following the news that some schools were banning skipping because they considered it dangerous, other schools hired people to teach skipping to pupils who no longer knew how to do it.

The Times/Daily Mail

Children from the Yarm Preparatory School, near Stockton-on-Tees, pointed out to teachers that the new road sign outside said, Grammer School Lane. It was hastily replaced.

Daily Mail

Ian Pettifer used a class of children to help him pop the question to his girlfriend, teacher Mel Fuller of Beedon School in Thatcham, Berkshire. He got down on one knee while the children held up cards spelling out: W-I-L-L Y-O-U M-A-R-R-Y M-E-?

Daily Telegraph

Pupils at White Hart Lane School in Tottenham, North London, speak fifty-eight different languages. Staff at the school hail from thirty-three countries and they teach 1,000 youngsters from more than fifty countries. Head David Daniels says, 'It's normal to be different here.'

Sun

During the 2005 celebrations to mark the anniversary of Nelson's victory at Trafalgar, a survey revealed that only one of the twelve children (aged 9 to 15) visiting Trafalgar Square knew who the man was on the top of Nelson's Column. Some thought it was Nelson Mandela and one 13-year-old thought it was 'the man who invented Wellington boots'.

Sunday Telegraph

'The test Eton pupils will want to pass most – fingerprint entry to the bar.' *Sunday Times* headline on a story saying that *Big Brother* has arrived at Eton, demanding that boys take a fingerprint test before using the sixth-form bar, which has a two-pint limit.

The Eton Wall Game – described as an impenetrable spectacle – has been played by prime ministers, princes and – possibly – by Jack the Ripper. But in July 2005 a 239-year-old no-girls tradition was broken. Eighteen teenage state-school girls on a course at Eton struggled to master the complex rules of a sport renowned for its indiscriminate violence and almost total lack of goal scoring. In spite of the gender barrier being broken, some things never change. The result was yet another 0–0 draw.

Sunday Telegraph

A survey found one in three people admitting that they had bought a book 'solely to look intelligent'. One in eight young people confessed to choosing a book 'simply to be seen with the latest short-listed title'.

Guardian

Teachers complained of a litany of bad behaviour, including pupils throwing stones, flooding toilets and setting off fire extinguishers. The complaints came from Sunday schoolteachers who also reported young worshippers climbing over pews and throwing or tearing hymn books. Scripture Union, the leading Christian publishing house, has published guidelines suggesting a system of yellow cards and sending parents on 'children's behaviour courses'.

The Times

From 1 November 2005, new migrants to Britain had to face twenty-four questions before qualifying for citizenship. A training day for teachers was held at Chester University, and only one of twenty who took the test passed it.

As people complained that the citizenship quiz was too hard, the *Guardian* asked its readers, Did YOU know:

- That you could dial 112 as well as 999 to reach emergency services?
- That Crown Courts are the only ones to sit with a jury?
- The dates of St David's and St Andrew's Days.

The 5-year-old daughter of Jim Parkinson, from Hessle, East Yorkshire, announced that she had been given the clap at school. It turned out that she had been given the plaque for good behaviour.

Daily Mail

'An hour of Elvis a day'

Chapter 17

Plain Eccentric

Sunflowers grow bigger if exposed to Elvis...

A *Times* correspondent from Warwickshire told of his late father always carrying an umbrella as part of his 'uniform'. He was seen caught in a heavy shower between the bus stop and his house – running home carrying the umbrella under his coat to keep it dry.

The Times

Donald McLachlan was the first editor of the *Sunday Telegraph*. A measure of his eccentric outlook is indicated by his suggestion that blind TB Utley be appointed as its TV critic.

Daily Telegraph

Britain's tallest MP, Tory Daniel Kawczynski, six foot eight and a half inches, is campaigning to have the height of the nation's doors increased.

The Times

In August 2005, 6ft 9 in tall Graham Boanas waded across the River Humber for charity. His feat inspired a letter from Richard Buxton of Totnes, Devon, telling how his late father Rufus Lord Noel-Buxton (a 6ft 3in socialist peer) waded the river in 1953. Dressed in grey-flannel trousers rolled up to the knee, checked shirt, canvas plimsolls and carrying a Scout staff, he waded the one and a quarter miles from Brough Haven in Yorkshire to Whitton Ness in Lincolnshire. He sought to demonstrate the possibility that Roman legions waded the river, joining up the Ermine Street, London-to-York route. He was sustained by a cigarette and a nip of brandy halfway. A crowd greeted his arrival with a shout of 'Sign him up for Scunthorpe. 'E's got stamina.'

Daily Telegraph

Daily Telegraph columnist Sam Leith remembers trying to phone playwright Harold Pinter, who won the Nobel Prize for Literature in 2005. He got through to Pinter's wife, Lady Antonia Fraser – 'one of the most charming women you will ever get on the phone.'

Leith asked whether Harold was in. She said that he was.

'May I have a word with him?'

'Sorry,' said Lady A. 'You've come through on my phone number. You need to phone him back on his own line.'

'I don't seem to have that number. Could you tell me what it is?'

'I'm afraid not,' she said. 'Bye.'

Daily Telegraph

Alan and Valerie Day – possibly the most determined queuers in the history of eccentric British queuing – spent four nights sleeping in their chilly car during freezing temperatures, snow and high winds. The 70-year-old retired bank manager and his wife saw in the New Year 2006 under a duvet, determined to be first in the queue to rent beach hut No. 84 on Avon Beach in Christchurch, Dorset.

The hut measures 6ft x 4ft, has no electricity or running water, and is rented by the local council for £705 a year. It can be used only from sunrise to sunset and from Easter to September. Said 63-year-old Mrs Day, 'Who wants to go to Spain when you can come here?'

Daily Telegraph

Once the preserve of retired couples with cardigans and Thermos flasks, the traditional British beach hut has become a status symbol for the middle classes. Even the most basic huts can command prices of over £100,000.

- In August 2005 a beach hut on Mudeford Sandbank in Dorset went on the market at £140,000.
- In October, a wooden chalet overlooking the sands of Embleton, Northumberland, sold for £100,000.
- In Abersoch, North Wales, a stretch of dune with planning permission for a 10ft x 12ft hut sold for £63,000.

Daily Telegraph

Civil servant Alan Binnie, 21, was approached by a passer-by who asked him, 'Do you want to kiss my fish?' – and then slapped him in the face with it.

Mr Binnie told Falkirk Sheriff Court, 'I ran into the police station and they asked me what I was doing with fish scales sticking to my face.'

David Evans, 22, was jailed for six months for this and other offences.

Daily Telegraph

Physicist Niels Bohr had a horseshoe hanging outside his cottage and was asked if he believed it brought him good luck. Bohr is said to have replied, 'Of course not, but I'm told it works whether you believe or not.'

Hal Ewing, Luton, Bedfordshire,
The Times

Following a patently ridiculous but 200-year-old tradition, dozens of people put their safety at risk to chase cheese wheels down a 1-in-2 incline at Cooper's Hill, Gloucestershire, in May 2005. Three contestants were taken to hospital and organisers said they were delighted that the number was so low. 'A lot less injuries than we'd normally expect,' said one.

Guardian

Richard and Anne McCowey live in a village near Newcastle – and spend their holidays visiting Newcastles around the world. There are fifty-four of them and their ambition is to see every one. Over the last five years, they have been to Newcastles in Australia, South Africa, Canada, America, Wales, Scotland and Staffordshire. Richard is 58 and a psychiatric nurse and Anne is 57 and a semi-retired nurse.

Newcastle Evening Chronicle

Kamikaze pigeons

Chapter 18

Service Life

A gathering of Wing Commanders is a flush of WCs...

In August 2005, the army created a stir by announcing that today's modern soldiers were to be issued better-quality underwear. Many readers' letters followed with memories of the unlamented old-style 'shorts cellular'.

Paul Hammond, of Torquay, Devon, wrote, 'I regret that the recent correspondence... is of little interest to those, like me, who served in a Highland regiment.'

Daily Telegraph

Roger Alford, of Guildford, Surrey, recalled the main characteristics of army-issue underpants (drawers, cellular, green): 'They came in two sizes – too big and too small.'

The Times

Todd Dunn, of Ferndown, Dorset, remembers that during his time in the Navy bad behaviour due to alcohol came in three categories: junior ratings were drunk, senior ratings were confused, officers were high-spirited.

Daily Telegraph

After London Marathon star Paula Radcliffe stopped for a very public pee during the 2005 event, Commander Geoff Marshal, of Gosport, Hampshire, wrote to the *Daily Telegraph* about the time he had to accompany a naval rating to court. The rating was charged with relieving himself in a public place and was fined. Later, he was awarded consequential naval penalties for bringing the Service into disrepute and being absent from duty while attending court.

Daily Telegraph

Ken Bratton, of Linlithgow, West Lothian, was serving on a ship when a rating [sailor], for a wager, dived from the top of the mast and then swam back to reboard. He was charged with:

• Leaving the ship without permission.

• Boarding the ship without permission.

Daily Telegraph

During World War II, American servicemen in Britain were referred to as 'overpaid, oversexed and over here'. But in November 2005 the National Archives revealed details which suggested that the GIs might be forgiven for the oversexed bit. They were, it seems, led astray by 'young British sluts and goodtime girls'.

The Times and other papers

The Americans became irritated by the overpaid, oversexed and over here taunt, and responded by pointing out that British troops were 'underpaid, undersexed – and under Eisenhower'.

Paul Callan, SW10, *Daily Telegraph*

During World War II, thousands of young British women found the vast army of US GIs billeted in the UK irresistible. The jokes and the catchphrases of the time say it all.

- Heard about the new utility knickers?
  One Yank and they're off.
- Army girls (ATS) were known as
  'officers' groundsheets'.
- Navy girls: Up with the lark and to bed
  with a Wren.
- The Women's Land Army motto 'Back
  to the Land' became 'Backs to the Land'.

In the midst of the amorous welcome they received, the GIs had the nerve to complain that British condoms were too small for their erections.

Sunday Times

The *Sunday Telegraph* carried correspondence about the way the British like to say that it was Winston Churchill, Tommy Handley and Vera Lynn who won the World War II for us. This was followed by a letter saying: 'Everybody knows it was my dad who won the war.' Signed Tommy Atkins (Jnr), Glastonbury, Somerset.

Sunday Telegraph

The role of three prostitutes who nursed casualties aboard HMS *Victory* has been commemorated with a limited edition of a special rum called Trafalgar Women. *The Times* under the headline 'Tarts with Hearts toasted with Trafalgar Rum'.

'I was treated like dirt at Sandhurst,' said Prince Harry on his 21st birthday in 2005. 'It did me good.' He added that he was looking forward to having Prince William salute him when his elder brother eventually joined Sandhurst.

Daily Telegraph

Major General Andrew Ritchie, the 52-year-old Commandant of Sandhurst, said he didn't treat Prince Harry, or any other cadet, like dirt. 'Officer cadets are all treated the same... If they don't get something right, they are told very clearly that they got it wrong... People are shouted at. That's something many young people haven't been used to. The regime at Sandhurst is gruelling... It comes as a hell of a shock.'

Prince William is expected to join Sandhurst early in 2006, and Maj. Gen. Ritchie comments, 'Knowing Prince Harry he will find an excuse to come back here so that Prince William has to salute him. That would make a good photograph. I think I might take that one myself.'

Sunday Telegraph

The Times parliamentary sketch writer Anne Treneman suggested that the collective noun for a group of generals in the House of Lords might be 'a glory'. This was followed by David Cogan, writing in from Farnham Common, Buckinghamshire, to say that during World War II a gathering of wing commanders was usually referred to as 'a flush' of WCs.

As part of the nationwide celebrations marking the 200th anniversary of the Battle of Trafalgar, *The Times* published reproductions of the newspaper's coverage of the historic event. Although this took up most of page one on Thursday, 7 November 1805, room still had to be found for a full column of classified ads. Alongside a dramatic dispatch from Vice Admiral Coillingwood, Commander in Chief of His Majesty's ships and vessels off Cadiz, there were advertisements such as:

- LOST, an OLD POINTER DOG, white with red spots, answers to the name of BASTO; almost blind, one eye quite gone. Any person bringing the said Dog to No.158, Swallow Street, Piccadilly, shall receive ONE GUINEA Reward and reasonable expences (sic) paid.
  – N.B. No greater Reward will be offered.
- A FINE MARE to be SOLD, the property of a Gentleman, warranted sound; walks, trots, gallops, and leaps remarkably well. To prevent trouble, the price is 40 guineas.

The Times

Captain Chris Craig RN (retired) recalls that some years ago he had the job of inspecting a Royal Navy destroyer in a simulated battle. The ship's command team were performing well, so he increased the pressure by quietly inviting the commanding officer to feign taking a mortal wound – leaving his team leaderless.

When the CO collapsed, a first-aid party appeared quickly. 'As the sailors were about to administer assistance, a glacial and firm voice cut through the quiet: 'Nobody... I repeat, nobody... is to kiss me!'

The Times

'England Expects That Every Man Will Do His Duty' was the famous message flagged from the *Victory* at the Battle of Trafalgar. Under the headline 'England Expected A Lot', J. Wood of Blackpool, Lancashire, writes: 'Serving on board *Victory* were twenty-two Americans, nine West Indians, seven Dutchmen, six Swedes, four Italians, three Frenchmen (all volunteers), three Norwegians, three Germans, two Swiss, two Portuguese, two Danes, two Indians, one Russian and one African.'

Daily Mail

World War I's Christmas truce occurred on 25 December 1914, when British and German troops crossed No Man's Land, shook hands, sang carols and played football. One of the last veterans involved in that truce died in Scotland in November 2005, aged 109.

Former Black Watch sergeant Alfred Anderson, of Newtyle, Angus, used to say that his ambition was to die shot in bed by a jealous lover.

Daily Telegraph

About 2,000 Spitfires were named after the generous organisations which helped to finance them. They included Dog Fighter (Kennel Club), Flying Scotsman (LNER) and The National Federation of Hosiery Manufacturers' Associations.

Len Sutton, Horncastle, Lincolnshire, *Daily Telegraph*

What should a Scotsman wear under his kilt?
In Highland regiments, not a thing – unless the Jock is performing Highland dancing in public. Black Watch sergeant majors used to walk behind the ranks on parade, raising kilts with their swagger sticks to make sure that bare bums, not wimpish knickers, were exposed under there. Anybody wearing knickers was removed from the parade ground without his feet touching the ground.

Philip Howard in
The Times

Chapter 19

Nanny State

6-year-old boy is asked for documentation to prove he is under 21...

After visiting Sunningdale Ladies' Golf Club, a health and safety official said the sand pits would have to be fenced in. The sand pits to which the official referred are known to golfers as bunkers.

Ephraim Hardcastle, *Daily Mail*

Teachers at a school in Norwich were told to make sure that pupils threw snowballs only if they were 65ft apart. And sledges were not to be used down hills.

Daily Mail

Police called in to investigate the vandalising of stained-glass windows at Middleton Parish Church near Rochdale didn't get close-up pictures of the damage because 'they didn't have specialised ladder training'.

Daily Mail

A government-backed booklet called 'Towards a Non-Violent Society' warned nursery teachers that playing musical chairs was 'not fair' and encouraged aggressive behaviour.

Daily Mail

Scottish schools were told that football matches with a score of 5–0 or more must be restarted at half-time with the score returned to 0–0 to prevent the losing team being humiliated.

Daily Mail

Following a failed attempt by a supermarket chain to change Spotted Dick into Spotted Richard, school computers in Norfolk began filtering out a pantomime project because the word Dick appeared along with Whittington.

Guardian

This story was followed by a comment in *The Times* the next day from Mark Brackenbury, of Dunmow, Essex, saying that presumably the question which computers must now answer is: 'Who killed **** Robin?'

Educational publishers Heinemann airbrushed out the cigar which engineering genius Isambard Kingdom Brunel was smoking in a picture they wanted to use. *The Economist* asked, 'Why stop at Brunel?' Running through a BBC list of top Britons the magazine pointed out:
  • Churchill drank too much.
  • Princess Diana was an adulteress.
  • Darwin lost his faith in God.
  • Shakespeare left his wife.
  • Newton dabbled in alchemy.
  • Elizabeth I had her enemies bumped off.
  • John Lennon took drugs.
  • Nelson fornicated.
  • Oliver Cromwell had nasty warts.

Economist

An Ipswich primary school bans hot cross buns in case they offend pupils who are Jehovah's Witnesses.

Observer

South Shields Council in South Tyneside lopped off the branches of six chestnut trees, fearing that children might hurt themselves climbing to collect conkers or throw sticks to dislodge them and hit passing cars. Local MEP Martin Callan called it 'the nanny state gone mad'.

Newcastle Evening Chronicle/Sun/Guardian

South Shields Council said it would eventually fell the chestnut trees and replace them with a less dangerous species.

Sunday Times

Norwich City Council cut down horse chestnut trees over concerns that falling conkers might hit pedestrians.

Daily Mail

An attendant at a public lavatory in Taunton was banned from jollying the place up with plastic flowers – in case they fell on patrons and injured them.

Independent on Sunday

Tracey Barnes from Claverham, Somerset, was told by the Passport Office that she could not use a photograph of her 9-month-old baby son because it showed him bare-chested.

Daily Telegraph

Daily Telegraph reader Fred Ogg wonders how children of his generation ever lived to tell the tale. His long list of things they survived included:
- We were born to mothers who smoked or drank – or both.
- We had no childproof lids on medicine bottles.
- We rode our bicycles without helmets.

- We drank water from the garden hose.
- We built go-carts from scrap and rode them downhill without brakes.
- We fell out of trees, got cut, broke bones and teeth and there were no lawsuits as a result of these accidents.
- We had unpasteurised milk and cheese, ate worms and drank soda pop with sugar in it.
- We weren't overweight because we were always outside playing.

'Daffodils Too Big a Danger for Taxmen' – *Daily Telegraph* headline on a story about Inland Revenue officials in Stroud, Gloucestershire, turning down the offer of professional gardener Jenny Bailey to brighten up her local tax office with a few daffodils. The officials quoted health and safety regulations and said that Mrs Bailey might hurt herself and sue.

Julie Scott got a phone call from the school in Weston-super-Mare attended by her daughter Emily, aged 9, saying that the girl had cut her finger and asking would she please come to the school, bringing a sticking plaster. Teachers wanted Emily's mother to apply the sticking plaster because under new health and safety rules they were not allowed to do it for pupils in case any of them were allergic to latex.

Experts said later they had never heard of a severe reaction to a sticking plaster.

Sun

Richard Littlejohn wondered if Nelson would ever have won the Battle of Trafalgar if he had been bound by modern health and safety regulations. This was after an actor playing the part of the illustrious admiral during celebrations commemorating the battle's bicentenary was forced to wear a life jacket.

Sun

The local council in Bexhill and Rye ordered some 1,000 'dangerous gravestones' to be pushed over so that they would not collapse on people. It was then told that the flattened memorials were still a hazard, as visitors might trip on them.

The Times

Amid all the stories of political correctness and nanny-state rules in Britain, Steven Edwards and his family moved to Spain to escape it all. He reported what fun it was among 'the pot-holed roads, dodgy kerbs and fiestas and fireworks in the streets'. His son's school has a three-strikes-and-you're-out policy 'and he behaves himself'.

Daily Express

For twenty-five years, Warwickshire firemen have had a Guy Fawkes night bonfire next to their station. It was banned in 2004 for breaching new safety regulations.

Daily Mirror

After complaints to the police at Bedmond, Hertfordshire, Kirsten Griffiths, 40, put a T-shirt on a nude garden gnome.

Sun

The escapades of Humpty Dumpty, Simple Simon, Jack and Jill, the Grand Old Duke of York and other nursery-rhyme characters expose children to ten times the violence of early-evening TV says a tongue-in-cheek study from Bristol Royal Hospital for Children. *The Times* ran a leader on 'How to Make Some Traditional Songs More Contemporary', including:
Jack and Jill went up the hill
To fetch a pail of water,
Jack fell down and broke his crown,
And Jill came tumbling after.
But there is no need to worry,
Surely no cause to fret,
A NHS Direct team caught them
With a giant safety net.

The Times/Sun

When MPs voted to ban fox hunting, *The Times* asked, 'Will the Ban Stand the Test of Time?' and reminded readers of earlier bans:

- Kilts – banned after the Battle of Culloden in 1746 in which the kilt-wearing Bonny Prince Charlie was defeated by the English army. They remained outlawed for thirty-six years.
- Christmas – abolished in 1652 by Puritans who thought it a Catholic superstition. It was decriminalised a few years later.
- Homosexuality – any homosexual act between men was outlawed in 1885 and repealed in 1967.
- Speeding – in 1865, the Locomotive Act restricted horse-less vehicles to 4mph in the country and 2mph in towns. (One person had to walk ahead carrying a red flag.) Repealed in 1896.

The Times

Motoring commentator Jeremy Clarkson has been told that all the trees in his garden must be doctored to stop children being able to climb them. This sparked him off blasting new European legislation which means councils will have to spend taxpayers' money checking that no playground roundabout can revolve at more than 11mph and slides must be altered so they're not too steep.

Sun

Hot on the heels of its Christmas warning about tripping over presents and being scratched by tree needles, the Royal Society for the Prevention of Accidents moved in on Shrove Tuesday and warned of the dangers of tossing pancakes. It issued safety guidelines and said around 250 people would need hospital treatment after taking part in the fun in 2005.

Guardian

Following a health and safety risk assessment by Wiltshire County Council, Abbeyfield Secondary School in Chippenham banned footballs from the playground. The kids then resorted to playing the game with empty Coke bottles.

Sunday Telegraph

St Anne's Primary School in Greater Manchester banned pencil cases after a pupil was injured with a letter opener brought into the school inside a pencil case. 'We banned them,' said the school, 'to prevent any other potentially harmful instruments being brought into the classroom.'

Sunday Telegraph

The story of Cinderella is being used in Hampshire as part of a pioneering scheme to teach children at primary and infant schools about their rights. The lessons tell children about the United Nations Convention on the Rights of the Child. At Portway

Junior School, pupils were asked what they thought about the way Cinderella was treated. 11-year-old Grace replied, 'Her stepmother was very cruel and denied Cinderella her right to be protected from abuse and it infringed Article 31 when they didn't let her go to the ball because children have a right to play.'

Daily Telegraph

An Oswestry primary school banned Punch and Judy on the grounds that it was too violent. *Sun* **columnist Richard Littlejohn wondered if the only acceptable modern version would be for Mr Punch to be put on the sexual offenders register and his lady given a place in a battered wives hostel, with the baby taken into care and then adopted by a gay couple.**

Sun

When Bradley Beaton went to his local bus station in Middleton, Greater Manchester, to get a junior bus pass he was told he must produce a birth certificate or his passport to prove that he was under 21. Bradley is 6 and his stunned mother said, 'He still has his baby teeth.'

Daily Express

There were those who were nervous about celebrating the anniversary of Trafalgar in 2005 because it might upset the

French. But in a letter to the *Daily Telegraph* Lord Tebbit said that a French friend once told him that no one could understand France without knowing that schoolchildren were taught that Trafalgar was 'an inconclusive naval battle in which an English admiral was killed'.

During the hottest days of the summer of 2005, residents of Leamington Spa, Warwickshire, clubbed together to buy an inflatable paddling pool for their children and put it up on a communal green. But Warwick District Council banned the children from playing in the 10ft-square, 12in-deep pool because there was no lifeguard. The ban was eventually lifted after parents were told to put up six signs saying the council would not be liable for any injury.

Daily Mail

This story followed others which appeared in many UK papers telling of games of conkers being banned in schools because they were considered too dangerous; homemade cakes being banned from a school fete in Wiltshire for fear of food poisoning; hanging baskets taken down in Bury St Edmunds in case they fell on someone; the back stroke being banned in a Lancashire pool to prevent swimmers crashing into each other, and a London school which stopped pupils making daisy chains in case they picked up germs.

Fife Council banned bouncy castles after accidents on ones owned by the council. The Royal Society for the Prevention of Accidents thought the council had over-reacted, saying, 'In all types of play, children get hurt.'

The Times

The maternity unit at Calderdale Royal Hospital in Halifax, West Yorkshire, has banned visitors from cooing over babies, claiming that such behaviour infringes their human rights. One ward there has a doll featuring the message: 'What makes you think I want to be looked at?'

A member of the hospital's special care baby unit said, 'Cooing should be a thing of the past because these are little people with the same rights as you or me.'

The Times/Halifax Courier

If you think we live in a nanny state today, have a look at what nanny was saying to us years ago. Over the last sixty years, public information films have advised the British on everything from How to Survive Nuclear War to How to Blow Your Nose. The National Archive is digging out these films and putting them online. Some examples:

Coughs and Sneezes Spread Diseases. A 1945 Ministry of Health film featured a middle-aged man being taught how to use a handkerchief. 'Close your eyes,' he is told. 'Now. Handkerchief. Sneeze. Sneeze, handkerchief. That's the idea.'

The Modern Guide to Health, shown in 1947, advised on the benefits of fresh air, exercise and wearing a coat in cold weather. Men were told how to sit properly on their office chairs. Instructions for women included: 'Let's see what you have to do during the day. There's breakfast to get ready. When you've got father off to work and the children off to school, there's the washing up to do. Then housework, ironing, cooking, another meal, more washing up... After putting the children to bed, there's father's meal to prepare, and more washing up. When that's done, there's always plenty of mending...'

Independent

Health and safety rules were also responsible for the Highland Park whisky distillery in the Orkneys having to do without its traditional mouse hunter. This followed the death in 2006 of Barley, a ginger tom who was the last in a long line of cats drafted in to hunt mice.

The Times

Bristol City Council spent £5,000 planting 100 yew trees – then dug them up after deciding they could poison children. But expert Trevor Beer and others said a human would have to eat several handfuls of the mildly toxic leaves or berries to trigger a serious reaction. If all Britain's poisonous plants were banned, they said, 'there would be no countryside left'.

Sun/The Times/Daily Mail with a headline: 'Yew couldn't make it up'.

Chapter 20

A Touch of Class

**'How long has your family lived at
your present address? "697 years,"
replied Sir Thomas Ingleby...'**

The great class divide lives on. When comedian
Ronnie Barker died, aged 76 in October 2005,
many newspapers chose to remember the classic
class skit he did with John Cleese and Ronnie
Corbett. Elegantly tall Cleese stands in line with
less elegant and chubby Barker and the tiny
Corbett in ill-fitting raincoat.

Cleese, with bowler and rolled umbrella, says of
Barker, 'I look down on him because I am upper
class.'

Barker, with trilby and collar and tie, says, 'I look

up to him because he is upper class. But I look down on him [Corbett] because he is lower class. I am middle class.'

Corbett, with flat cap and muffler, says, 'I know my place. I look up to them both. But I don't look up to him [Barker] as much as I look up to him [Cleese], because he has got innate breeding.'

The class system remains a permanent fixture, according to a long-term study by the Office for National Statistics. The social class into which you are born remains the best indicator of where you will stay for the rest of your life. Falling down the social ladder is a rarity and family background is a definite predictor on how well a child does.

A London School of Economics expert says that, despite attempts to improve social mobility, allowing people to succeed on their own merit, it still largely depends on the position into which you are born.

The Times

The Reform Club once dismissed a highly prized chef who had been 'found with a housemaid'. Club members then held a mass meeting to demand his reinstatement – with rights over all the housemaids.

From *The Gentlemen's Clubs of London*,
by Anthony Lejeune (Parkgate Books).

An official form asked Sir Thomas Ingleby how long his family had lived at their present address. His accurate answer: 697 years.

Observer

(Sir Thomas lives at Ripley Castle, Yorkshire. Henry Ingleby collected taxes for Edward III and helped the King to finance the construction of Windsor Castle. Sir William Ingleby served Henry VIII, Mary Tudor and Elizabeth I.)

It's a story which brings to mind the American visitor who asked a member of the English landed gentry how the family managed to keep their lawns in such immaculate condition. 'Just roll and mow them for three or four hundred years,' he was told.

Gentlemen's clubs in Pall Mall and St James' allow members to wear corduroys – but taxi drivers using ranks at Lowestoft and Great Yarmouth railway stations have been warned that wearing corduroy trousers could cost them their licences.

Daily Telegraph

Corduroy's place in the fashion stakes has been a matter of debate for years, and the *Telegraph* followed up its Lowestoft story with conflicting views:

- 'Often linked to dishevelled, Left-leaning polytechnic lecturers in sandals,' writes David Sapsted.

- Famous wearers include Stephen Fry, Alan Bennett and Michael Palin. The longer you have them, the better they look.' Jeremy Hackett, founder of the upmarket men's clothing brand.
- 'The fabric of English country life that unites all classes.' Christopher Howse.

Daily Telegraph

The Duchess of Cornwall's former husband, Brigadier Andrew Parker Bowles, once proudly carried the ceremonial silver-headed staff that signified his rise to Commander of the Household Cavalry and so-called Silver Stick in Waiting to the Queen – 'a title Andrew would not find even faintly ridiculous'.

Victoria Moore, *Daily Mail*

Victoria writes that a friend of Andrew's says, 'He is rather proud that his ex-wife has married the future King of England.'

Daily Mail

A correspondent asked why the sound of people whistling is seldom heard these days.

This was followed by Christopher Cox, of Warnham, West Sussex, saying that only delivery boys on bicycles 'had the annoying habit of whistling in public. A gentleman should whistle only for his dog.'

Daily Telegraph

There are some 100 concierge companies operating in the UK and having a personal lifestyle manager is becoming commonplace for the super rich. Here are some of the requests they have had to deal with:

- Madonna wanted her favourite herbal teabags flown in from America.
- Jennifer Lopez asked for a dozen albino peacocks for a cocktail party.
- One client needed a psychiatrist for her cat.
- A wealthy lady hired a naked male cleaner for the day.
- A couple paid £20,000 to fly their dog from America in a private jet with a minder.

Daily Mail

Council re-paints yellow lines

Chapter 21

Council Daze

Come to Peckham and see the graveyards...

Extracts from a council's tenants' complaints department:

- Please send someone to mend the garden path. My wife tripped on it and now she is pregnant.
- The toilet is blocked and we cannot bath the children.
- Our lavatory seat is broken and we can't get BBC2.

Reg O'Donaghue, SE17, *Daily Mail*

Bath & North East Somerset Council is advertising for a dormouse officer. It expects the successful candidate to 'identify dormouse heritage', hold 'dormouse-related activities' and promote 'intellectual access and enjoyment' to dormice.

Daily Mail

A housing development in St Fillans, Perthshire, had to be relocated because locals believed that fairies live on the original site. The Planning Inspectorate stated solemnly that it had no specific guidelines on fairies, 'but local customs and beliefs must be taken into account'.

The Times

A Leeds woman has reported a witch doctor to the West Yorkshire Trading Standards Office because his spells didn't work. She wanted the man of magic to bring her partner back and his advice included slaughtering three cows and floating some of her pubic hair down the local River Aire.

Yorkshire Post/Evening Post, Leeds

An unemployed man with thirteen children, a wife and a live-in lover says his four-bedroom council house in Allenton, Derbyshire, is too small. He wants a bigger one but the local council says he already has the biggest house they've got available. The family get £2,000 a month in benefits but he thinks the council has failed him. 'I think this country is going down the pan,' he said.

The Times

There were no yellow lines in Sheepcote Street, Birmingham, when drivers parked their cars there one day in March 2006. But workmen came along and painted yellow lines around their vehicles – and £60 parking fines followed. The council backed off after victims complained of a jobsworth mentality.

The Times

The story reminded the *Birmingham Mail* of an earlier jobsworthian incident when Santa Claus was ticketed as he delivered presents to a children's hospital in the city.

And there are stories from across the country about people being fined for putting their bin bags out for collection on the wrong day or in the wrong place. Others have been collared for putting the wrong kind of rubbish in street litterbins.

Birmingham Mail

British local councils come in for a lot of stick over stupid, stubborn bureaucracy, but they have a long way to go to beat this one from Australia.

'Your local council will give you a special ruler to measure the exact distance that your colour-co-ordinated garbage bins must be placed from the kerb (get it wrong and the bin men won't pick them up).'

Amanda Platell (an Aussie herself)
in the *Daily Mail*

An overzealous traffic warden slapped a ticket on a mobile blood transfusion van while office workers were inside donating blood. Sutton Council, Surrey, cancelled the fine.

Teletext

The website also recorded the case of a motorist in Westminster who got a ticket for parking under an illegible sign – from which all the letters had fallen off.

AppealNow.com

Welsh lollipop lady Debbie Roberts was told that she could not help children across Graig Road in Newcastle Emlyn, Carmarthenshire, because the traffic there was too dangerous. Children spent six weeks fending for themselves before the local council bowed to pressure. 'What do you expect our children to do? Sprout wings and fly across the road?'

Western Mail

Lambeth Council has spent hundreds of pounds creating a seating area in Brockwell Park exclusively for the use of the borough's drunks.

News of the World

Traffic wardens confessions:
- I often patrol the area surrounding the ground of my favourite football club, targeting the vehicles displaying the away team's sticker.
- We run a weekly sweepstake for 'most expensive car of the week nicked'.
- If there is a minute or two left on the meter, I often engage drivers in conversation until their time is up.

Sunday Telegraph magazine

The local council in Bath has come up with a money-saving idea. Force motorists to drive more slowly by not bothering to repair potholes.

News of the World

A politically correct Cornish Borough Council had signs reading Hitler's Walk taken down. Mevagissey parish council asked for them back because they were in memory of a 1930s councillor who was nicknamed Hitler because it was his job to ensure that fishermen paid their harbour dues.

Daily Telegraph

The London Borough of Southwark has issued a glossy tourist map aimed at highlighting the delights of Peckham, which often hits the headlines as a hotspot for crime, shoddy public housing and the location for shady goings on in TV's *Only Fools and Horses*.

It's all unfair, say the burghers of Peckham, and their map invites visitors to amble through one of London's finest Victorian graveyards, marvel at the award-winning Peckham Library and feast on a bacon butty at the Bubble 'n' Squeak café.

Famous sons of Peckham include Boris Karloff and Anton Ferdinand, the West Ham and England Under-21 footballer, along with his older brother Rio, of Manchester United and England.

Anton Ferdinand says, 'The place has changed since I was a kid. I'm proud to come from here.'

Del Boy Trotter once said in *Only Fools and Horses*, 'I thought the only people who missed Peckham were the bloody Luftwaffe.'

Independent

A passenger in Matthew Buer's car dropped the remains of his 80p bag of chips out of the window on the outskirts of Colchester. The chips landed in Tendering and the council there sent Mr Buer notice of a £50 fine. The chip bag landed just over the border into Colchester Council's area – and Mr Buer duly got a second £50 fine notice from that council.

Daily Telegraph

Andy Tierney, 24, had a £50 fine slapped on him for putting two pieces of junk mail into a street litterbin. Hinckley & Bosworth Council said the fine was because he had used the bin to dispose of 'domestic refuse'. Critical newspaper stories followed and the fine was withdrawn.

Scotsman/BBC News/Sun and others

Jon Henley's Diary in the Guardian runs a 'thankfully occasional' feature called Provincial Parking Problems, which has called attention to:

- A street in Norwich where 116 parking permits have been issued for fifty-eight spaces.
- Villagers in Mottram, Lancashire, being told that dozens of potholes will not be repaired because they provide 'an effective traffic-calming scheme'.

Guardian

Chapter 22

Let Us Pray

'We have an array of bedroom accessories, such as handcuffs,' Ann Summers spokesperson...

Abigail, a *Daily Mail* reader's granddaughter, was talking about her daddy when her friend, Josie, said, 'I haven't got a daddy.'

Abigail asked, 'Has he gone to live with Jesus?'

'No,' replied Josie. 'He's gone to live with Sandra.'

Daily Mail

There was general astonishment over the speed with which Cardinal Ratzinger was chosen to be the new pope in April 2005. *Independent* columnist John Walsh thought the best pope joke was the revelation by his colleague Miles Kington that the German cardinal won the vote so smartly because he rose early and, with Teutonic cunning, put his towel on the papal throne before anyone else was awake.

Independent

After officiating at a wedding in the Plymouth area, a vicar turned up at an evening celebration in Looe, Cornwall, wearing a T-shirt carrying the message: 'Vicars do it kneeling down'.

Daily Telegraph

A West Midlands church was told by Dudley Council that it would need planning permission to erect a cross on its new building – on the grounds that the universal Christian symbol is classified as an advertisement.

Observer

The Best Parish Pump Misprint Award run by the satirical Christian website ShipofFools.com was one which surprised worshippers at a traditionally abstemious Lake District Baptist church. Their church magazine invited them to a meeting 'that will be gin with prayer'. Second place went to a church where 'speaking' was misspelled and the service sheet read: 'Teach us, Lord, the art of spanking'.

The contest was in memory of printer Robert Barker, whose 1631 edition of the Bible had the Seventh Commandment as 'Thou shalt commit adultery'.

Ruth Gledhill in *The Times*

'It's just called *The Bible* now – we dropped 'Holy' to give it a more massmarket appeal.' Quote from publishers Hodder & Stoughton.

Financial Times

Lenn Budd, the publisher of a book entitled *The 100-Minute Bible*, was asked: 'Is it a dumbing down?' He replied, 'Yes, but that's the world today... the Bible is very user-unfriendly. People just don't have time to read it. If this book means more people can answer pub quiz questions on the Bible, so much the better.'

Guardian

After *The 100-Minute Bible*, the *Sun* decided to reduce some all-time classics to just one line:
- *Hamlet* – Self-absorbed nutter bangs on about death.
- *War and Peace* – French invade Russia, French retreat from Russia.
- *Pride & Prejudice* – Woman fancies rich bloke, then goes off him, then decides to marry him.
- *Lady Chatterley's Lover* – Posh bird romps with gardener.

The Bible has been translated into text-message language. Look forward to: 'In da Bginnin God cre8d da heavens and da earth... God luvd da ppl of this wrld so much dat he gave his only son so dat every1 who has faith in him will neva really die.'

Daily Telegraph

A statue of St Anthony of Padua – patron saint of lost things – has disappeared from All Souls Church in Peterborough.

Independent on Sunday/
Peterborough Evening Telegraph

A long correspondence about getting to sleep by using variations on the old method of counting sheep included a letter from the Rev. A. J. Birch claiming that he found rehearsing his next sermon to be an effective method. Neil Ardiff, of Dublin, followed this by saying that maybe the Reverend's congregation should try to recall his last sermon when they have problems nodding off.

Guardian

Under the headline 'There's no such thing as a perfect sermon', an article in the *Sunday Telegraph* said, 'For a vicar, a perfect sermon would stirringly convey the profundity of religious truth and the beauty of God's work. For a congregation it would be, well, short.'

The article ends with advice on how to keep your

spirits up when the address is less than divine. It includes:

- Hat-counting. In these days of fewer hats, include purple rinses.
- Sermon Cricket. Score a run every time the preacher uses a personal pronoun, a six when he waves both hands and a wicket every time he says 'God'.
- Stained-glass Sudoku. Count the panes of stained glass in each window.
- Sermon Alphabet. Listen for words beginning with each letter of the alphabet until you get to Z. The lack of gospel texts on xylophones means you might have to wait a while.

Sunday Telegraph

The Rev. John Banner, of Tunbridge Wells, urged Christians to object to an Ann Summers outlet and a spokesman for the shop said, 'We are predominantly a lingerie retailer, but we do have an array of bedroom accessories such as handcuffs.'

Daily Telegraph

Nearly eight out of ten people in Britain do not know the name of the Archbishop of Canterbury, reported a poll commissioned by *The Times*. Some believed that the Church of England's top archbishop was Pope John Paul II.

The Times

Under the Data Protection Act, chaplains find it difficult to get details of hospital patients. The Rev. David Ackerman, of Kempsford, Gloucestershire, wonders if the way forward might be:

- The hospital cites the Data Protection Act.
- Patients cite the Human Rights Act to assert their right to see a chaplain.
- The chaplain cites the Freedom of Information Act to see patients' details.

Daily Telegraph

The Roman Catholic Church has instructed priests to stop praying for sick parishioners by name, fearing that they may be prosecuted under the Data Protection Act.

Daily Telegraph

Three pagan inmates of Portsmouth prison are visited by a pagan priest who is allowed to take in his tarot cards and a wand – but not the cauldron he uses in spell-making.

Daily Telegraph

The Venerable Gerry Hollis was once an inspirational parish priest in the Sheffield area – and an accomplished sportsman. He died, aged 86, and after his obituary appeared in the *Telegraph* in January 2006, George Horne, of Escrick, York, wrote, 'The obituary

brought back happy memories of when we both played in the village cricket team. A Saturday wedding didn't stop him playing. After the service, he would cycle to the ground and whip off his cassock to reveal immaculate whites underneath.'

Daily Telegraph

Chapter 23

Mind Your Language

Boots chemists 'Dispense with accuracy'...

In the early part of 2006, a fierce debate developed over the use and abuse of the apostrophe. Some argued that we should stop using them altogether. In the *Guardian*, Robert Adams of London pointed out that Kingsley Amis was once challenged to create a sentence whose meaning depended on an apostrophe. He came up with: 'Those things over there are my husbands.'

This was the apology Richard Brinsley Sheridan made when told to apologise for calling a fellow MP a liar: 'I said the honourable member was a liar it is true and I am

sorry for it. The honourable member may place the punctuation where he pleases.'

John Hamilton, Orpington, Kent, *Guardian*

After it was reported that Dolly Pentreath, who died in 1777, was believed to be the last person to speak Cornish as her first language, a reader pointed out that the language did not become extinct until 1782. 'Dolly predeceased her parrot by five years.'

Daily Telegraph

British Airways is doing its bit to kill off the old joke about the UK and the USA being divided by a common language. In a bold initiative to make US travellers feel at home, it has created the first online dictionary of English–English. But the *Independent* thinks the dictionary could give the Yanks a very strange picture of England in the 21st century – a world where taxi drivers still call you 'Guv' and people routinely offer you a 'cuppa cha'.

'The BA slang lexicon displays a bizarre bipolarity of class – mixing cockney sparrow talk with aristocratic yapping... and wartime RAF words like "barmy" and "chinwag"... The notional American tourist is urged to say "hols" and "tickety-boo" as if he were Bertie Wooster.'

John Walsh in *The Independent*

A leaflet for a Spanish financial group claims: 'You will be professionally attended, offering you all our know-how and services, to satisfy all your finantiall needs. And because we know how important ist to be understand, the whole team is well trained in English.'

Spotted by *Daily Mail* reader Peter Thompson

English may be the liveliest and most flexible language in the world, but Adam Jacot de Boinod has trawled dictionaries around the world to discover unlikely words that other languages have but English does not:

- **Baku-shan – A woman who looks better from behind. (Japanese)**
- **Nakhur – A camel that won't give milk until its nostrils are tickled. (Persian)**
- **Tingo – To borrow objects from a friend's house, one by one, until there is nothing left. (Easter Island)**
- **Queesting – Admitting one's lover to one's bed just for a chat.**
- **Magandang hinaharap – Admiration for a woman's breasts. *The Times* says this is a phrase which can be translated as 'Phwoar!'**

The Times reviewing *The Meaning of Tingo*, published by Penguin

In the Welsh version of Scrabble there is no Q or Z – but there are tiles with LL and DD and the opportunity to score 164 points with the Welsh word for 'necessity' – angenrheidiaeth.

The Times

Many years ago Boots ran an ad with the phrase: 'Boots dispense with accuracy'.

Eric Blakeney, Cheadle, Cheshire, *The Times*

During November 2005 there was a running correspondence in the *Guardian* about the meaning and distribution of the word 'cludgie'. For many, it meant lavatory, and was/is widely used in Scotland – with some claiming that it meant an outside lavatory.

Roy Love, of Sheffield, remembered a Clyde boarding house listing its main improvement for the year as 'Cludgie Seat Revarnished'.

Guardian

Mark Pattison, of Blackburn, got a Japanese keyboard which included a list of old favourite tunes. Many had suffered by being first translated from English into Japanese – and received further torture when translated back from Japanese into English. Here are some which Mr Pattison asked *Daily Mail* readers to identify:

- Do you think old England's done?
- Ease up Mother Brown.
- It's raining, but I'm singing.
- My coconuts are lovely.
- Stand next to your man.
- Too many sleepy people.
- Mulberries round the bush.

Daily Mail

The Friends of Norfolk Dialect group has successfully lobbied for schools to teach the 'wonderful, rich local dialect' which includes:

- He'yer fa' got a dickey, bor? (Has your father got a donkey, boy?) To which the correct reply is: Yis, an' he want a fule ter roid him, will yew cum? (Yes, and he wants a fool to ride him, will you come?)
- Do we go play on the titty totty tittermartorter? (Let's play on the very small see-saw.)
- I've got the uppards and downards. (I've got diarrhoea.)

The Times

The Avon and Somerset Police Force went trendy to get its message across to anti-social youth in Bristol. Their posters were written in text-style patois which baffled many of the older residents. For instance:

- D bil cum arnd hre n will vzit ur olds if u r messin about. Translation: 'The police patrol this area and will pay your parents a visit if they find you are misbehaving.'
- Du ur olds know whr u r o wot u r doin coz D bil wl tel em. Translation: 'Do your parents know where you are or what you are doing? Because the police will tell them.'

Daily Mail

Neighbourhood watch

Chapter 24

Golden Oldies

**Old-age pensioner wheel-clamped while
sitting in his car...**

A reader of the *Independent* asked Joan Rivers,
'What are the pitfalls of dating in your seventies?'

She said, 'When you have to decide whether to
spend your money on a vibrator or a pacemaker,
life becomes very difficult.'

Independent

Two of the last British soldiers left alive after serving
during World War I were guests of honour at the National
Army Museum in November 2005. They gave very
different prescriptions for long life:

Bill Stone, 105, swears by clean living, a contented
mind and trust in the Lord.

Henry Allingham, 109, said he was blessed with a sense of humour and put his longevity down to 'cigarettes and whisky and wild, wild women'.

Daily Telegraph

Scarborough Council withdrew a guide for pensioners about obtaining benefits after its title raised some local eyebrows: 'Are You Getting It?'

Daily Telegraph

Gillian Rogers, of Eastbourne, wrote that, as she approached her 80th year, she was wondering whether prison might not be the best place to be. 'Heating bills paid, three meals a day, free dentistry and medical treatment, no responsibility and I might even get free computer classes.'

Next day G. R. Wells of Romsley, West Midlands, reminded Gillian Rogers that from next year (2007) prison will be one of the very few places where she can enjoy a smoke under cover.

Daily Telegraph

The *QE2*, the *grande dame* of the seas, reached her 36th birthday in May 2005 and is sailing towards retirement. Sad news for 85-year-old widow Beatrice Muller who has lived on board for five years, paying £3,400 a month. She has travelled more than half a million miles and spends her time 'dancing, playing bridge and trying not to eat'.

The Times

Ronnie Ronalde remembers how Frank Sinatra and Marilyn Monroe were among his greatest fans when he was billed as the greatest professional whistler in the world. On his 82nd birthday, the *Daily Mail* reported that Ronnie had plans to tour Britain in 2006. 'Nowadays,' he said, 'I get a lot of requests to whistle at funerals.'

The *Marshwood Vale Magazine*, circulating in West Dorset, South Somerset and East Devon, reported the 103rd birthday (on Christmas Eve 2005) of James Noel Webber. Mr Webber (Jim) told them, 'I didn't learn a lot at school, but for two years I went to evening classes at Cheddington village hall. The classes were planned for Wednesdays, but this was my courting night... so the classes were changed to Thursdays.'

Jim says he still works practically every day, looking after six gardens in the village. 'When I'm feeling a bit under the weather my daughter Kathy makes up my drink of sugar, generous whisky and a drop of milk topped up with hot water... I read mostly without spectacles, but need them for driving. My new driving licence is valid until 2008.'

Pensioner Eric Martin was wheel-clamped while sitting in his car in Loughborough town centre. He had no idea it was happening as he sat waiting for his wife to return from shopping and was startled by a parking attendant knocking on the car window and asking for £80 to release the clamp.

Daily Telegraph

Prince Charles may talk to his plants – but Winston Campbell, 77, of Great Torrington in Devon, says his secret for becoming a champion cactus grower is playing Dolly Parton records to them.

Sun

Chapter 25

Just the Job

**Insurance worker gets damages after falling
over a pile of accident claim forms...**

A Glasgow man stripped naked while questioning a
woman job applicant and later explained in court that
it was all part of his 'tough interviewing technique'.

Independent on Sunday

A joke they tell in insurance circles got an outing in the
Daily Mail. Six insurance companies amalgamated and a
shield of arms was commissioned to mark the event. The
Herald responsible for the design explained that the six
sections of his shield represented:
1. Man in bed with wife – Legal and General
2. Man in bed with fiancée – Mutual Trust

241

3. Man in bed with secretary – Employer's Liability
4. Man in bed with prostitute – Commercial Union
5. Man in bed alone – Scottish Provident
6. Baby – General Accident

Submitted by John Mathews,
Llaanllwch, Carmarthen, *Daily Mail*

Pet lovers take more time off work to look after their sick animals than they do for poorly relatives. In two years, 2.7 million working days were lost because pets were ill – but only a million for sick family. (Direct Line Pet Insurance survey.)

Daily Mirror

Stephen Masty, of SW London, wrote to *The Times* saying that he had just recently sworn an oath and become a British citizen. 'Where now,' he asked, 'can I complain about all the foreigners who come here taking our jobs?'

The Times

During an office clearance of old ledgers in Edinburgh, a 60-year-old document was discovered showing the starting salary of one guinea a week for a 14-year-old boy employed as 'a barrow worker'. The name on the document is Thomas S. Connery, later better known as Sean.

Daily Telegraph

Plumbers give the worst value for money and provide the worst quality of service of all tradesmen.

Scottish Construction News
reporting the results of a survey

The above item prompted a repeat of stories from the *Daily Telegraph* printed in an earlier edition of *You Couldn't Make It Up*:

My grandmother asked a plumber to attend to a severe leak last Wednesday, but was told that was the day he put aside for golf. He came the next day in his soft-top Mercedes.

Charlie Longe, London SW11,
Telegraph

My plumber's bill for half an hour's work was £100. I protested that I was a solicitor and couldn't charge at that rate. He replied, 'I know – I couldn't either, when I was a solicitor.'

Telegraph

Insurance worker Linda Riley, from Newburgh, Scotland, got £5,000 damages after she fell over a pile of accident claim forms at work.

The Times

Guardian readers have been tracking down cute business names.

A hairdresser in Nether Edge in Sheffield is called Edge Cutters, another one sent in from Cumbria called Curl up and Dye; a fireplace business named Grate Expectations; a sports equipment shop called The Merchant of Tennis; in Wales trees are trimmed by The Special Branch; in Leeds a tanning salon called Tanz In 'Ere; and in East Ham a baby clothes shop – From Here to Maternity.

Guardian

In January 2006, the *Sun*, under the strapline 'You Couldn't Make It Up', began to hunt for 'Britain's biggest jobsworths and bird-brained pen pushers'. It filled page 13 with these three examples:

- Officials from Rotherham Council in Yorkshire swooped on a couple who were feeding birds and fined them £50 for dropping litter.
- A primary school at Stow-in-the-Wold, Gloucestershire, cut meatballs from its menu in case pupils choked on them.
- For decades the Royal Mail has delivered post to the remote hamlet of Cefn Minog in the Black Mountains, South Wales (population: four). But deliveries have been axed by Mail chiefs who say that a stile

and a dirt track leading to the hamlet could
be lethal for postmen.

Christmas kiss

Chapter 26

Christmas Presence

**Mary told Joseph that Jesus had been a
'right little bugger all day'...**

Santa Claus has become a victim of political
correctness. In October 2005, some senior Santas
got together to discuss their image and draw up a
Code of Conduct. Among the things they decided
were:

- Beards must be six inches long.
- Stomachs must meet regulation
  portliness – with waists between 46 and
  48 inches.
- All Santas must be able to say 'Hello' in
  ten different languages.
- They must never smell of alcohol.

247

- They must know the names of
  all the reindeer.
- They must have sufficiently red cheeks.
  ('But not too red. We don't want them
  looking like drag queens.')

Daily Telegraph

Bethlehem's maternity services left nothing to chance if a school Nativity play is anything to go by. Mrs C. A. Durrant, of Crawley, West Sussex, heard her son practising one song which had Mary and Joseph in the barn with 'the oxygen standing by'.

Daily Mail

During a school Nativity play, the baby Jesus, as usual, was represented by a large plastic doll. When Mary picked up the doll, it announced in a loud American accent, 'My diaper needs changing'.

From *A Wayne in a Manger*, by Gervase Phinn
(Michael Joseph). *Daily Mail*

Dorset Police are imaginative in their undercover operations. In the summer of 2005, they patrolled a troublesome stretch of beach in skimpy trunks. In December, they wanted to make a surprise drugs raid so they approached a suspect house disguised as carol singers resplendent in Victorian costumes. Beneath their cloaks were stab-proof vests and their friendly hound was a sniffer dog. A woman who came to the door offered them a pound to go away, but the wassailing officers went straight in and made two arrests.

Guardian, under the headline
'Merry Christmas – you're nicked'

Around 1905 the Beecham Company published its own book of Christmas carols, including:

Hark the Herald Angels sing
Beecham's pills are just the thing
For headache strong, for stomach mild
Two for adult, one for child.

This was sung on the streets according to the clergyman grandfather of Simon Sholl of Oxford.

Daily Telegraph

Maroussia Richardson, of Exeter, remembers another verse of the Beecham carol, which she sung, gleefully, in about 1948:
If you want to go to Heaven
Just take six or seven
If you want to go to Hell
Why not swallow the box as well?

Daily Telegraph

Telegraph contributor Ian Bradley referred to a 1937 version:

Hark the Herald Angels sing
Mrs Simpson's pinched our King

Linda Hall, of Shepperton, Middlesex, reports that Liverpudlians had their own pastiche of 'We Three Kings':

We four lads of Liverpool are
John in a taxi, Paul in a car
George on a scooter, pooping his hooter
Following Ringo Starr.

Daily Telegraph

Philip Armstrong, of Bodle Street Green, Sussex, told of his daughter's version:

We three Kings of Leicester Square
Selling ladies underwear
How fantastic, no elastic
Only a penny a pair.

Daily Telegraph

Former Prime Minister Ted Heath, who died on 17 July 2005 aged 89, won the award of The Man Most Least Likely to Dress Up as Santa so many times that he was allowed to keep the trophy.

Sunday Times

George McAllister, 42, a professional clown and Santa, was caught driving at 100mph on the M90. At Perth Sheriff Court in October 2005, he asked to be allowed to stay on the road at Christmas so that he could visit children in hospital. Sheriff Robert McCreadie limited Santa's disqualification to two months, on top of a £350 fine.

McAllister said later that 'The Sheriff Who Saved Christmas' would be getting a nice present from Santa.

The Times

Birmingham Council renamed Christmas as Winterville to avoid offending other religions or ethnic minorities.

Sun

The Make Poverty History campaign wanted their Santa Claus to deliver thousands of cards to No. 10 Downing Street. But they say they were told Santa could not do that because he was a man in disguise. Hugh Muir in the *Guardian* commented, 'Special Branch is much maligned these days, but you can't say those officers don't know their stuff.'

Keith Waterhouse tells his favourite story of how the infants of a North Yorkshire village acted out the Nativity play in their own words. Joseph clomps in from the fields and asks, 'Nah then, our Mary – how's our little Jesus?'

Mary: 'Ee, Joseph, he's been a right little bugger all day.'

Daily Mail

Was there a cat in the stable where Jesus was born? The question popped up in Celia Haddon's highly entertaining pets column in the *Daily Telegraph* and C. L., of Truro, Cornwall, responded, 'Of course there was – a tabby cat. When Jesus began to cry the tabby soothed him back to sleep with its purring. Mary traced her initial on the cat's forehead and ever since this mark is found on every tabby.'

Daily Telegraph

Celia's column digs deeper into the 'Animals in the Manger' question and says that a few Christmases ago the Fancy Rat Society produced a cover for its magazine showing rats worshipping the infant Jesus. 'I think we can be sure,' writes Celia, 'that there were rats in the manger. Why else would the tabby have been there?'

Daily Telegraph

It's the office Christmas party – and time for the tipsy tradition of photocopying naked bums. A survey of Canon's technicians found that one-third of their work over Christmas involved repairing broken glass that had been sat on – or fixing paper jams that revealed embarrassing images. Canon is increasing the thickness of the glass on its machines to cope with the extra load of what repairmen now call 'rear-end copying'.

The Times

Eating mince pies is illegal. Oliver Cromwell banned them – and anything to do with gluttony – in the 17th century and the law has never been repealed.

Sun

When she was four years old, Jean Coles was photographed kissing Graham Packham (about the same age) underneath the mistletoe. When she was sixty-two, Jean came across the picture of that kiss – illustrating a Christmas card on sale in a Bristol Tesco. The 1947 image had been in a picture library until Tesco commissioned it for one of their 2005 Christmas cards.

Jean became a postwoman and now lives in Knowle, Bristol. Graham is a retired vice principal of a further education college and lives in Hebden Bridge, Yorkshire.

Jean said, 'I remember the picture being taken. Graham was holding a box of Smarties. When I asked for some he refused and I burst into tears.'

Graham said, 'This has made my Christmas.'

There is talk, now, of a reunion.

Daily Telegraph

A copy of the world's first Christmas card was auctioned for £2,999. The 1843 card shows a family toasting an absent friend and was criticised by some Victorians for encouraging drunkenness.

The Times

Politically correct government departments put Season's Greetings on their Christmas cards instead of Merry Christmas.

Sun

Prince Charles always does his Christmas cards early in October.

Daily Telegraph

Chapter 27

Transports of Delights

**Flight is delayed 'because air traffic controller
is on his tea break'...**

During a spell of hot weather in June 2005, London
Tube passengers were urged to show more
consideration for other travellers. They should take
a shower before journeying, said an executive of
the Underground.

Daily Telegraph

A wonderful British attitude was revealed on *The Times*
leader page following a story that many UK rail journeys
now take longer than they did two decades ago. There
is now ample time to admire bucolic scenery from train
windows, the ironic leader said. 'Why hurtle from

Portsmouth to Southampton in thirty-five minutes, as our hectic forefathers did in 1898, when today's trip takes a far gentler forty-six minutes? The old BR 125 dizzied passengers at speeds that left little time for lunch... It now averages a sober 61mph from London to Norwich... chefs have plenty of time between Ipswich and Diss to toss a salad to perfection.'

The Times

When the engine of a Midland Mainline train from St Pancras to Nottingham broke down, the driver asked if passengers had any sticky tape. No one had and the train was delayed for almost an hour and a half before finally terminating at Leicester.

The Times

When Nigel Baker's train was late arriving at Paddington, it was announced that the delay was due to excessive boarding at Reading. Mr Baker, of Tibberton, Gloucestershire, asks if fare-paying passengers have now become 'just a tiresome barrier to the smooth running of the railways'.

Daily Telegraph

There was a prolonged correspondence in *The Times* about why one always travels UP to London, even when travelling from North to South. What was surely the final word came from the Rev. Jonathan Jenkins: 'It is entirely possible, during engineering works, for trains to be transferred between tracks, so that an up service travelling down south might be heading uphill on a down line at the same time as a down service travelling up north is heading downhill on an up line.'

The Times

Why buses come in threes.
They leave the depot at timed intervals. The first picks up lots of passengers at the first stop. By the time it sets off again, the second bus is getting nearer and there are now fewer passengers at the first stop and it takes less time to pick them up. The same happens until the two buses end up running together. On long, busy routes they can be joined by a third.
From a book by scientist Richard Robinson on the *Science of Murphy's Law* available from the *Sun* Book Shop.

Sun

'Transport Direct' – a government website – offers door-to-door travel directions in Britain. But some of its suggested routes are unnecessarily long and expensive – and one of them would require walking on water across the River Clyde.

The Times

Journey by a London Bus (1950) featured two African students marvelling at the punctuality of British transport and the way passengers form an orderly queue.

Independent

Passengers on a flight from Tenerife spent an extra twenty-five minutes in the air while waiting to land at Cardiff Airport. 'Sorry,' said the pilot. 'The air traffic controller is on his tea break.'

The Times

Chapter 28

What's in a Name?

A step-by-step guide to elementary bottom pinching...

The village of Bell End in Worcestershire was voted as the place with the rudest name in Britain by UKTV viewers. It came in ahead of Twatt (Orkney & Shetland), Three Cocks (Powys) and Six Mile Bottom (Cambridgeshire). Bell End is not far from Lickey End.

Sunday Times

Any viewers baffled by the choice of Bell End could turn to Google and read about the bulbous tip of the protuberance, the old chap, the tallywhacker, Little Winston, the one-eyed trouser snake, the gentleman's downstairs, fowling-piece, tadger, kidney-nudger.

Gentleman's English Dictionary

Newspapers find rude place names irresistible. In August 2005, the *Daily Mail* had a two-page spread under the headline 'The Rudest Places to Live'. They included:

- Sandy Balls in the New Forest, Hampshire.
- Scratchy Bottom, along the Dorset coastal path.
- Slag Lane in Haydock, Merseyside.
- East Breast in Greenock Docklands.
- Back Passage in London E1.

Extracted from *Rude Britain* (Boxtree) by Rob Bailey and Ed Hurst, which explains the ancient origins of these comic place names.

Daily Mail

Residents of the small Austrian town of Fucking got fed up of British tourists pinching their road signs and considered changing its name. Eventually, they decided to keep it and the mayor said, 'After all, Fucking has existed for over 800 years.'

Sunday Times

The *Sunday Telegraph* suggested that Fucking might appropriately be twinned with Intercourse in Pennsylvania, or Condom in France or Climax in Colorado.

Sunday Telegraph

There is a place called Bacon's End near Solihull. I never go there.

Jon Bacon, Harrietsham, Kent, *Daily Telegraph*

When Wyllan Horsfall Oberwald, of Sheffield, was asked for his name in a hospital accident ward, he was told, 'Not the accident. Your name.'

Daily Telegraph

Jack Woodford, of Buckfastleigh, Devon, who lives at 5 Avery Close, received a letter addressed to 5a Very Close.
Daily Telegraph

Zog Ziegler, who lives at Severn View, Haw Bridge, Gloucestershire, has received mail addressed to 7 View, Whore Bridge.

Daily Telegraph

Port Isaac in Cornwall has a Squeezy Belly Alley.
Christopher Piggins, Salisbury Wiltshire,
Daily Telegraph

More than half the people in Britain don't know the names of their neighbours and a third would avoid them in the street. Research by Linden Homes, a house building company, found that 60% would mumble a hasty hello and then move on if confronted with a neighbour.

The Times

The 2006 shortlist for the *Bookseller*/Diagram Prize for Oddest Title of the Year included:

- *Bullying and Sexual Harassment: A Practical Handbook* – taking the reader step by step through elementary bottom pinching and advanced innuendo.
- *People Who Don't Know They're Dead: How They Attach Themselves to Unsuspecting Bystanders and What To Do About It.*
- *Rhino Horn Stockpile Management.*

Independent

At a meeting of the parish council in May 2005, Councillor Fish was re-elected as chairman and Councillor Fish as vice-chairman.

Spotted by Barry Cooper, of Doncaster, Yorkshire, in the *Misterton & West Stockwith Parish News*

Today's celebrities who lumber their children with potty names have got a long way to go to match the old-timers of Cornwall. Archivists there combed records as far back as the 16th century and compiled a list of more than 1,000 names which sound preposterous, rude or hilarious today. They include:

- Faithful Cock
- Truth Bullock
- Bunnyface
- Susan Booze
- Edward Evil

- Charity Chilly
- Offspring

The prize for invention must go to Mr & Mrs Hornblower, good Baptists of Truro, who named their seven children Horatio, Azubia, Constantia, Jecoliah, Jedidah, Jerusha and Erastus.

The Times

A local estate agent found difficulty in selling off new retirement flats in Purley, near Croydon, after the block was named Purley Gates.

Guardian

The Purley Gates story was followed by readers' letters remembering retirement homes called Dyer's Court and others in Terminus Avenue (Bexhill on Sea) and St Peter's Close (Peterborough).

Guardian

Eclipse Lodge is the name of a residential home in Torquay and there's a George Bush Funeral Home in Norwich.

Guardian

The Women's Institute doesn't have chairwomen. Members who take the chair are addressed as Madame Chairman.

The Times

Architectural Mr Blobby

Chapter 29

Odds & Sods

A gentleman is someone who knows how to play the bagpipes – but doesn't...

An official of the World Toilet Organisation told its conference in Belfast that they were not 'taking the future of world waste sitting down'.

The Times

Women spend a year longer on the phone than men. The *Daily Mail* reported this result of a poll under the headline: 'Really, as little as that?'

In his *Daily Telegraph* column, Andrew Marr wondered why he can't get a cheaper haircut on the grounds of having hardly any hair. Reader Susan

Cokyll responded with the story of an almost bald friend who raised the same question with his barber and was told he was being charged a search fee.

Daily Telegraph

Following complaints about weather forecasters using folksy euphemisms, V. Ridley of London cheered up the *Sunday Telegraph*'s letters page by reminding readers of *The Two Ronnies* sketch:

Ronnie Barker: It will be dry in Rye.

Ronnie Corbett: It will be cool in Goole.

Ronnie Barker: And those of you living in Lissingdowne are advised to take an umbrella.

Sunday Telegraph

A friend heard the following exchange between two young shop assistants:

'Where did you go for your holiday?'

'Majorca.'

'Where's that?'

'Dunno – I went by plane.'

Daily Telegraph

A well-known TV weather forecaster who was seeking an upgrade on a British Airways flight asked a stewardess: 'Do you know who I am?'

She summoned a colleague and said, 'Can you help? This gentleman is having trouble knowing who he is.'

Ephraim Hardcastle, *Daily Mail*

Pop singer Mick Hucknall graciously told the purser on a British Airways flight that he would be happy to sign autographs. The purser replied politely, 'Whom should I say is offering?'

Sun

Lies, damn lies and official statistics. The Office for National Statistics says that nearly four people in ten believe official statistics. But, as that is an official statistic itself, six out of ten won't believe it.

The Times

Daily Telegraph commentator Tom Utley, 51, disclosed a long list of things which irritate him now that he is middle-aged:

- Disgusting Andrex adverts with the repulsive slogan: 'Could you be cleaner?' The monstrous impertinence of being invited to muse at the breakfast table on how thoroughly I have wiped my bottom.
- Your call is important to us.
- Thank you for not smoking.
- For my sins.
- Web page not found.
- You're welcome.
- Fat people walking very slowly three abreast along narrow pavements.
- Cold callers.

Daily Telegraph

Next day a *Telegraph* reader added his own list of things to excite rage in the middle-aged:

- Wearing a tie with the shirt top button undone.
- Leaving floral tributes at murder/accident sites.
- Cycling on pavements.
- Cars with open windows emanating loud noise masquerading as music.
- The Prime Minister smiling.

Anthony C. Payne, St Bees, Cumbria,
Daily Telegraph

It seems the North-South divide is still with us.

Alistair Campsie, of St Cyrus, Aberdeenshire, met a shepherd in Yorkshire who told him that Hadrian's Wall should be rebuilt... On the far side of Doncaster to keep the Southerners out.

The Times

The crystal ball of an amateur psychic studying botanics at Edinburgh University failed to predict that it would cause a fire which destroyed his and two other flats in the City's Marchmont area. Firemen said the fire was started by the ball concentrating a ray of sunshine on a pile of washing.

The Times

The Times readers debated the problem of getting their offspring to keep in touch when away from home. Suggestions included:

End your letter to them saying Cheque Enclosed – but don't enclose the cheque.

A rubber stamp for a boy at university which read: 'Date as postmark. Dear Mum and Dad, Still Alive. All is well. Love George.'

The Times

Two weeks in the Med exposes you to as much sun as a year in the UK.

Independent on Sunday

John Lewis, 65, wrote to the Post Office asking for a postbox for his housing estate in Leeds. His letter got lost in the post.

Sunday Telegraph

In his *Sunday Telegraph* column, Terry Wogan tells 'a true tale from a Sainsbury's Customer Service desk'.

A woman returns a disposable barbecue demanding her money back because 'It's full of coal.'

'What did you think would be in the box?'

The woman points to a picture on the barbecue box showing sausages, burgers and chops sizzling away.

'Did you buy one and get one free?' asked the assistant.

'Yes, the other one's at home in the deep freeze.'

Sunday Telegraph

Wogan also tells of a mother-to-be entering a store and asking to be directed to maternity wear.

'Sorry, I can't tell you that,' says the assistant. 'It's Sunday and we can't trade until 11am.'

'But I don't want to buy anything yet. I just want to know where it is.'

'Sorry, I can't tell you. It's the law.'

'Couldn't you point?'

'Sorry. You'll have to come back at eleven.'

Mother-to-be goes for a wander and returns after eleven. 'Now can you tell me?'

The assistant doesn't look up when she says, 'We haven't got one.'

Sunday Telegraph

Michael and Catherine Hopcroft had their gas cut off due to roadworks in their street at Trym, Bristol. They went to bed at 11pm and when they got up next morning found a 'Sorry we missed you' card from a Wales & West Utilities engineer who had called to reconnect them – at 3.35am.

Daily Telegraph

On Friday the 13th 2005, the *Independent* filled page 29 with stories about paraskevidekatriaphobia – fear of Friday the 13th. It said superstition required people to 'Bolt the doors, toss salt over your left shoulder and rub your lucky rabbit's foot... A child born today is doomed to misfortune. You shouldn't marry, move home or job, or feed anyone eggs laid this morning… Don't get your hair cut or a member of the family will die.'

Among those who have shared superstitious dread of the 13th are Napoleon, Mark Twain, Herbert Hoover, Winston Churchill and Franklin D. Roosevelt.

Independent

In the 18th century, the government tried to debunk the myth that ships sailing on a Friday would have bad luck. A vessel was commissioned and named HMS *Friday*. Construction began on Friday the 13th and a captain called Jim Friday was appointed. She set sail on a Friday… and vanished.

Independent

Paul Maxfield, an engineer from Stoke-on-Trent, went into a Las Vegas casino, beat 448 of the world's best poker players, walked out with $1.7 million and said, 'It's not luck. It's not gambling. It's psychological warfare.'

Paul always wears a shirt with a collar. It stops the pulse in his neck showing if he gets excited. He has dark glasses because no one can stop their pupils dilating if they get excited at a good hand. 'The rest is whether you can hold yourself together under severe pressure,' he says. 'Can you play a bluff from the heart as if you really have got two aces?'

Sunday Telegraph

The Loch Ness monster is not alone. Nessie-type monster sightings have been claimed in twenty-three other lochs and it is also an international phenomenon – with sightings reported from China, Russia and North America.

Guardian

Commenting on a report that one in five toddlers can open 'childproof' containers, Laura Smith, of Effingham, Surrey, wrote that a quick survey revealed that the proportion of adults was pretty much the same.

The Times

The Monopoly board game celebrated its 70th anniversary in 2005 and produced a limited edition called 'Here and Now'. The *Daily Mail* devoted a whole page to it under the headline 'Goodbye Park Lane, hello Canary Wharf'. It reported:

- Bank notes start at £10,000 and go up to £5 million – original denominations from £1 to £500.
- Players passing through Go get £2 million – up from £200.
- Regent Street costs £2.8 million – up from £300.
- Park Lane & Mayfair (£350 & £400) have been replaced by Canary Wharf and The City (£3.5 million & £4 million).

- The penalty for landing on Super Tax is up from £100 to £1 million.
- There is a penalty card ordering the player back three spaces because of the rush hour.

Daily Mail

Human cannonball fired because he is afraid of flying.

Todd Christian, 26, a lifelong daredevil, is not afraid of being fired 40ft above the circus ring at 60mph. It is long-distance aeroplane flights that bother him and he did not want to fly to Brazil for specialist training.

Mail & Guardian – Africa's First Online Newspaper and other newspapers around the world

As part of a 'dirt is good' advertising campaign Persil compiled a list of thirty-three things a child should do by the age of 10. Favourites included:

- Making sandcastles
- Climbing trees
- Making a den
- Rolling down a grassy bank
- Making mud pies
- Tracking down worms
- Collecting frogspawn
- Cycling through a muddy puddle
- Burying a friend in sand

- Playing Pooh sticks
- Making breakfast in bed for Mum and Dad.
  Playing computer games did not make
  the list.

Guardian/Daily Mail

Meet the most famous faces in history – the lookalikes who get paid for resembling famous people.

Actor Gerry George, of Ealing, West London, does Churchill and says, 'He was such a charismatic leader. Some people have tears in their eyes when they see me dressed as him.' Gerry also does George Formby.

50-year-old Maloviere – who likes to be known only by his surname – does William Shakespeare. The bard's spitting image, from Totnes, Devon, has appeared as Shakespeare on phone cards, stamps, mouse-mats and in films and says, 'When I walk down the street people shout things like 'Wherefore art thou'.

Former deep-sea diver Ray Hill, 60, of St Albans, Hertfordshire, does Einstein and says, 'When you dress as Albert Einstein people show you a great deal of respect.'

Retired teacher Ray Irving, 56, of Chorley, Lancashire, does Henry VIII and says, 'In a stately home once a woman said, "That's a good statue." I said to her, "I agree," and she nearly jumped out of her skin.'

Sun

The Eurovision Song Contest does not get a good press in the UK. Even commentator Terry Wogan said of the 2005 version, held in the Ukrainian capital of Kiev, that viewers were about to see 'the banal, the bizarre and the downright barking'.

Wogan quipped in the *Radio Times*, 'Usually I'm the worse for drink by about song seven... Britain won't win... We've invaded too many countries and nobody likes us.'

The Times/Telegraph/Radio Times

A Teletext survey reports that more than a million people in the UK get into a row every day over the TV remote control. Research shows that the gadget inspires every emotion from anxiety to fury:

- One in ten people have come to blows.
- 3% admitted they had used the handset as a weapon.
- 26% have hidden it away.
- 16% admit putting themselves in the way to block the signal.
- Changing the channel and messing about with the volume without asking were two of the biggest annoyances.

Western Mail

Powergen told its customers their power bills were going up and softened the blow... by offering them four free energy-saving light bulbs.

Sun

British pensioners living in Spain get £200 winter fuel allowance.

The Times

Jack Tripp, MBE, widely regarded as Britain's greatest pantomime dame, died aged 83 in July 2005. He took his role as seriously as a Shakespearean part and said, '*Mother Goose* is the *Hamlet* of pantomimes.' Tripp was described by *The Stage* newspaper as 'the John Gielgud of pantomime dames'.

The Times

Love lies bleeding? Twenty-five per cent of the membership of the Romantic Novelists' Association are unpublished.

Daily Telegraph

A *Sunday Telegraph* reader wanted to know how to reply when a grandson asks, 'What makes the world go round?' Suggestions from other readers included:
- God.
- Good deeds.
- If the child is not to become a precocious brat, say, 'Because it does.'
- Ask your mother.

Sunday Telegraph

More than 500 Birmingham residents had little or no water during July's hot spell in 2005. A resident complained, 'We can't have a bath or flush the toilet. Severn Trent Water seems to have washed their hands of us.'

Sunday Mercury

When a record-breaking 11,000 bagpipers gathered in Edinburgh in August 2005, *The Times* said that from a distance the noise they made sounded like a 'mass of tropical insects feasting on a carcass'.

None of the participants – including the New York City Corrections Pipe Band and the thirty-strong Pakistan Pipe Band – was likely to agree with the critic who once said that bagpipes were an ill wind that nobody played good.

The Times reported that never before had such a deafening drone been created and never before had so many people simultaneously chosen to ignore the old definition of a gentleman: 'Someone who knows how to play the bagpipes – but doesn't'.

The Times

People were happier during the 1930s Depression, according to research at Cardiff University's School of Psychology. It says that the most important ingredients for happiness are family relationships, family networks, a camaraderie bringing a sense of community and belonging. And a belief in God, any god.

The *Daily Mail* produced a list of '30 things about the 30s', including:

- Around 180 were murdered a year (800 now).
- There were 3,500 divorces in 1930 (167,000 a year now).
- A family home cost around £650 (177,000 now].
- The average weekly wage was £2.47 (£422 now).
- An Austin 12 saloon cost £235 (but today's Ford Mondeo is cheaper in real terms, at £15,900).
- The *Beano* comic was born in 1938.
- You could buy three stewing pigeons for half a crown.

But not everything changes. Falling potato sales were blamed on the fashion for slimming.

Daily Mail (which cost 1p back in the 30s)

Victoria Beckham was widely quoted as saying that she had never read a book. Later she told the *Daily Telegraph* this was nonsense. 'What I said in an interview with a Spanish magazine was that I never seem to finish books. I start them, get distracted and never seem to get time to finish.' The *Telegraph's* page-one headline on an inside feature was: 'I DO read books – but not to the end.'

Daily Telegraph

Next day the Daily Telegraph reported that Mrs Beckham was not alone. Former Tory health minister Edwina Currie said, 'If ever I am told that I don't have long to live, I might start *War and Peace*, knowing that I won't have time to finish it.'

Dorothy Parker wrote, 'This is not a novel to be tossed aside lightly. It should be thrown with great force.'

Groucho Marx once said, 'When I picked up your book I was so convulsed with laughter that I had to set it down. But one day I intend to read it.'

Daily Telegraph

Charity shops spend £4.5 million a year disposing of unsaleable donations such as dentures, books with missing chapters, single shoes – and even a coffin.

The Times

Things that happen only movies:
- If you start dancing in the street, everyone you bump into will know the steps.
- Detectives can solve cases only after they have been suspended from duty.
- The Eiffel Tower can be seen from any window in Paris.
- All beds have L-shaped sheets that reach to the armpit level on a woman

but only to the waist of the man lying
beside her.

David Randall's Curious World in the
Independent on Sunday, dipping into the
Nostalgia Central website

Beryl Bainbridge, the 70-year-old author of twenty-one novels and three works of non-fiction, said some of her books were short for two reasons. Publishers used to like short books because it used to cost more if you went over 200 pages. 'And anyway, I cut and cut and cut... There's a great saying by someone like Voltaire who wrote a letter to someone saying, "I'm sorry this is so long, I didn't have time to make it shorter."'

Guardian

For the crew of the Oban lifeboat, it is becoming something of a habit. For the third time since 1997, a baby was born on board while rushing a pregnant woman to hospital. After Rachel Holliday gave birth to a daughter on her way from the Isle of Mull to the mainland in October 2005, RNLI crew-member Jim Watson said, 'That's six I've had now. Three of my own and three on the boat.'

The Times

The Times backed up the Baby on Board story with other emergency births, including:

A girl born on a Virgin Atlantic flight at 30,000ft in March 2004. She was named Virginia and granted free flights until she is 21.

Annemarie Mitchell, 22, gave birth to a boy at her wedding reception in Newbury in 2002 while cutting the cake with her husband Jeff.

And You Can't Do Better Than a Kwik Fit Fitter. Victoria MacMillan went into labour while stuck in traffic with her husband George. They pulled into a Kwik-Fit centre in Stockport, where their baby was born.

The Times

The Wythit branch of the Women's Institute in Leeming Bar, North Yorkshire, have been pole dancing, visited a strip club, had a painting session with a male model and lessons in belly dancing. Average age is 33.

Yorkshire Post/Times

A Co-op near Bath refused to sell fireworks to Susan Field unless she could prove she was over 18. Ms Field is a 50-year-old grandmother.

The Times

Hamlet was being performed in Basingstoke, complete with SAS uniforms, helicopter sound-effects... and this interpretation of the plot in the programme:

Prince Hamlet thought Uncle a traitor
for having it off with his Mater;
Revenge Dad or not?
That's the gist of the plot and he did,
nine soliloquies later.

David Marwood, Basingstoke,
Hampshire, The Times

Advice on the plot of a Shakespeare play reached its nadir when I took my son to Stratford. An American student asked her teacher to explain what was happening. The response was: 'This is Shakespeare honey; no one understands Shakespeare.'

George Medd, *The Times*, under the headline:
'Bard To Verse'

Forty beautiful women contested the Miss West Lothian 2005 contest. The event was broadcast live, but only on *TalkSPORT* radio. The organiser promised that the girls taking part were gorgeous and *The Times* lamented, 'We'll have to take his word for it.'

Neil Heppel, of Solihull, West Midlands, tells of the hours of pleasure he got as a boy 'burling' a metal hoop

for miles in all weathers. He had a hoop made for his two sons when they were 10 and 12 and they were absolutely incredulous to learn that this had been his only toy. They were not at all interested in playing with it.

But Mr Heppel's hoop does not lie idle. He still gets it out and is treated with howls of derision as he burls up and down the road.

Daily Telegraph

When supermarkets get shopping lists online, they sometimes pack substitutes if the ordered goods are out of stock. David Waite, of Watlington, Oxfordshire, says that in his case Sainsbury's brought a whole new meaning to their slogan 'Try Something New Today'. Along with his delivery was a note saying: 'You ordered a nine-pack Andrex honey toilet tissue. We have delivered one Harpic Limescale Remover.'

Daily Mail

Listeners to BBC Radio 4 voted Prime Minister Blair the sixth most powerful man in Britain – alongside the boss of Tesco.

Guardian

Top of the poll was European Commission President Jose Emanuel Barroso. Rupert Murdoch came second and the Google search engine was eighth.

BBC

Amid all the pop stars and TV and sports celebs, the 2006 New Year Honours list remembered some vital people. The crimper responsible for styling the hair of Diana, Camilla and Charles became an OBE, and an MBE went to 65-year-old Brian Tipper, who ensured that Big Ben was accurate to within half a second on Millennium Night.

The Times

Chinese tourists flocked to Bicester Village to buy highly prized British shoes from Clark's... not realising that many of the shoes on sale there were made in China.

Daily Telegraph

Children who are fussy eaters should be starved for twenty-four hours and they will soon eat anything. Baby won't sleep? Smack it until it stops crying.

Advice given in early editions of *Nursery World*, which celebrated its 80th anniversary in December 2005.

But in 1926 the magazine told its readers, 'Mud pies are much more important than the keeping clean of a pretty smock.'

The Times

Guardian readers are a serious-minded lot who get to grips with the really important issues. After a series of readers' letters on what can be done with empty 35mm film canisters the Guardianistas switched to worrying about an alleged shortage of mint imperials. Loads of letters turned up revealing where this most English of sweeties can still be located, and these were followed with the query: 'How many mint imperials will a 35mm canister hold?'

Six, said Ian Morrey of Barlow, Derbyshire.

Seven, said Mandy Wragg of Todmorden, West Yorkshire (who added that her dad always had several in the glove compartment on long car journeys).

Eight, said Michael Fry-Foley, of Cricket Malherbie, Somerset.

I can fit nine, boasted Robert Corky of Dublin.

Guardian

Betty Lowe, of Andover, Hants, remembers mint imperials being known as 'granny's sookers'. In church, her father would pop one in his mouth when the sermon began. If the sermon lasted longer than the mint, it was considered too long.

Guardian

Was it George Bernard Shaw who had a shed called London, so that his maid could tell callers that he was away in London?

Andrew Marr, writing in the *Daily Telegraph* about the difficulties of getting a bit of privacy these days

When NatWest bank began removing clocks from the walls of their branches, customers claimed that it was so that they would not notice how long they had had to wait to be served.

Sun

A *Daily Mail* reader from Newquay writes, 'When my darling granddaughter was coming up towards 12, she persuaded me to stop smoking. She thought alcohol was "yukkie", hated swearing and thought telling lies was naughty.

'Now, at 16, she smokes like a chimney, drinks like a fish, swears like a trooper and lies at the drop of a hat.'

Daily Mail

David Belcher, of Chesham, Buckinghamshire, writes about his local Tesco introducing customer comment cards. He used them to complain regularly about the store's 'noise polluting music' and 'was so successful that it withdrew the cards'.

Daily Telegraph

Duncan Campbell's diary in the Guardian began a search for the perfect answer phone message. Arthur Harada wrote in from Chester to say that he once had his answer machine saying, 'This is the police. Arthur Harada is in custody. Please leave your name and number and we will get back to you.' He found that this cut down the number of messages dramatically.

Madonna continues to love London despite having clocked up £2,500 in parking fines.

Daily Mail

Rubber bands, used by the Royal Mail to hold post bundles together, are often dropped in the street by postmen. Collecting them has become something of a national pastime, 'a new sub culture'.

Bob Russell, Liberal Democrat MP for Colchester, uses his collection for bundling up newsletters. 'My record find is thirty-seven in one street in Colchester,' he says.

Royal Mail donated 20,000 to help make the world's largest rubber-band ball – which was eventually dropped from a plane to see how high it would bounce. Sadly, instead of bouncing when it hit the ground at 400mph, the ball created a 9ft crater.

The Times

While visiting the Fitzwilliam Museum in Cambridge, Nick Flynn tripped on a loose shoelace, fell down a staircase and smashed three Chinese vases worth around £100,000. He referred to the accident as his 'Norman Wisdom moment'.

Guardian

Show homes used by developers to sell new houses are sometimes tricked up to look far superior to the actual properties which will be built for sale. A report by New Build Inspections told of:

- Developers leaving all lights on to create an impression of more natural light.
- Using glass furniture and mirrors to provide a feeling of space.
- Removing internal doors to make the house appear larger.
- Fitted furniture being only half the normal depth.
- Using children's furniture to make rooms appear to have more floor space.
- Show homes finished to the highest possible standards, possibly by contractors different from those who will build the homes being put up for sale.

Daily Telegraph

The Publishers wish to acknowledge the following publications

Daily Mail
Daily Express
The Times
Daily Telegraph
Sun
Guardian
Financial Times
Independent
Scotsman
Metro
News of the World
Independent on Sunday
Sunday Telegraph
Observer Magazine
Observer Food Magazine (OFM)
Sunday Mercury
London Review of Books

The Press Gazette
Reader's Digest
Catholic Herald
Private Eye
Economist
Yorkshire Post
Birmingham Evening Mail
Newcastle Advertiser
Newcastle Evening Chronicle
Liverpool Daily Post
Evening Post, Leeds
Sheffield General Cemetery Trust Magazine
Brighton Argus
Coventry Evening Telegraph
Colchester Evening Gazette
Tamworth Times
Halifax Courier
Henley Standard
West Sussex Gazette
Western Morning News
Western Mail
Oban Times
Eastbourne & District Advertiser
Seaford Friday Ad
Cumberland News
Scunthorpe Target
Shropshire Star
Tandridge Chronicle
Radio Times

New Scientist
Country Life
BBC Olive magazine
Journal of Sexual Medicine
Adult Learners' Week
Focus magazine
Cambria magazine
Dogs Today
BBC News
Surrey Online
Teletext

You Couldn't Make It Up

'What a wonderful collection of old rubbish' – Keith Waterhouse

In his many years as a newspaper journalist, the inimitable Jack Crossley has stumbled upon literally thousands of wonderful little anecdotes that you really wouldn't believe if you hadn't seen them written down in black and white. He has compiled them into this irresistible book of essential whimsy.

Sir, While clearing the house of a deceased aunt we found a box labelled, correctly: 'Pieces of string too short to keep.'

Genuine letter to *The Times*

Our story about a fire being started by an old pouffe at No. 7 Douglas Cottages, as reported last week, referred to an item of furniture and not the owner, Mr Donnie McArthur.

Apology that appeared in the *Dunoon Observer*

ISBN 1 84454 005 7 • £6.99

You Really Couldn't Make It Up

After the runaway success of *You Couldn't Make It Up*, Jack Crossley presents his second cornucopia of wonderful anecdotes and strange goings-on from around the British Isles.

A Northumberland woman saw a TV tip about putting crabs in the fridge for 20 minutes before cooking them. She followed the advice – and the crabs ate ten choc ices.

Independent on Sunday

At the age of 105 Dolly Jackson , of Hereford, said that she started smoking when she was 14 – but was giving it up to help her live longer.

News of the World

ISBN 1 84454 078 2 • £7.99

You Absolutely Couldn't Make It Up

'All human life is here in twenty-six chapters of mirth ranging from British eccentricity to legal lunacy to royal flushes to saucy seaside humour'

From the mad machinations of the British bureaucrat to the one-off antics of barmy eccentrics who pepper our towns and cities, Jack Crossley's skill is in hacking a way through this bewildering forest of the pompous, predictable, polemical, political and pure pap to pick out the stories that really matter. The ones that make us laugh.

A sex survey claims that an orgasm burns off
27 calories, but faking it uses 160

Sun

A bookie in Putney, London, hired a feng shui
expert to redesign it's betting shop – because
punters kept on winning.

Mirror

ISBN 1 84454 180 0 • £7.99